Cute Owls

Adult Coloring Books

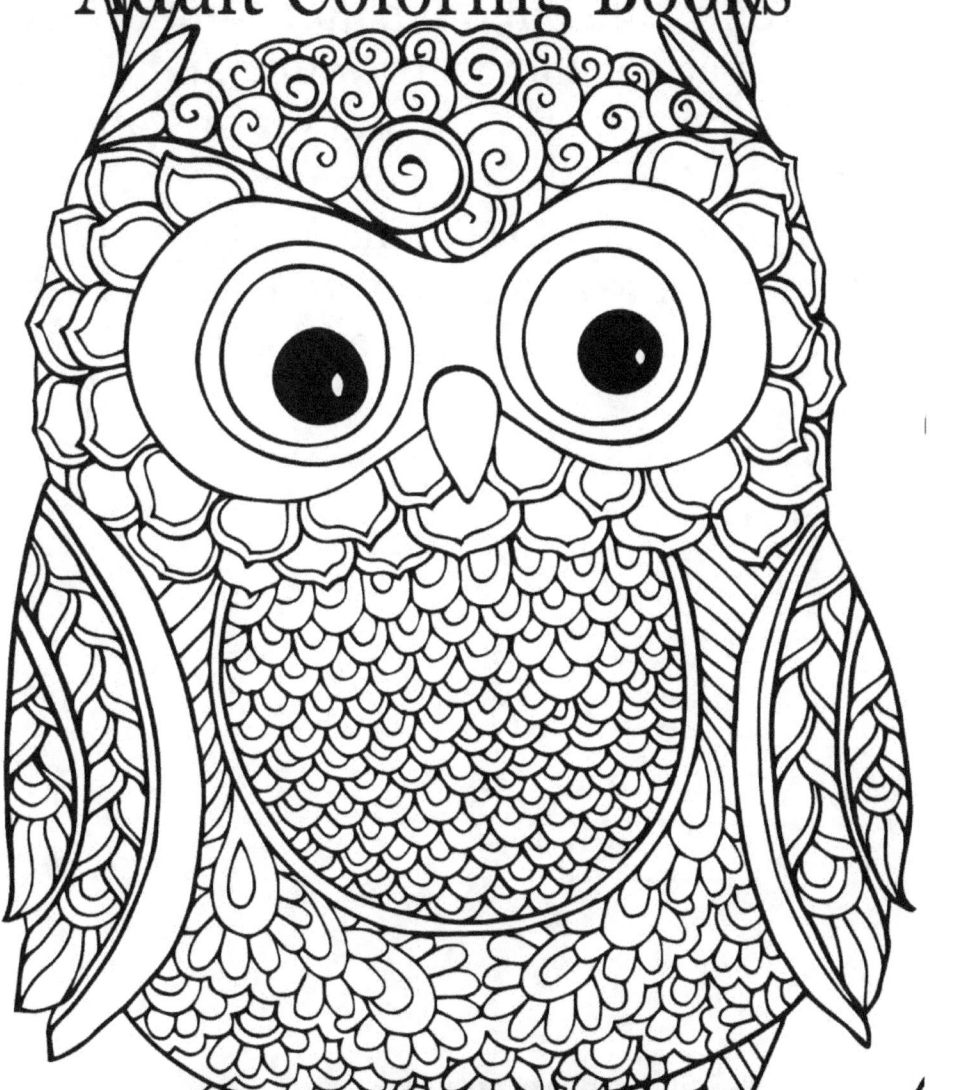

50 adorable hand drawn owls to color

Clara Hughes

Clara Hughes lives in Florida with her four cats, Fluffy, Tab, bunny and pepper. She loves to draw, and with a quirky sense of humor, her designs are not only cute but often quite humorous. Claras ink drawings are the perfect choice for young and old alike and are suitable for pencil, crayon, marker or water colors.

Cute Owls is a collection of adorable hand drawn owls. They all bear the common theme of cute and quirky and are the perfect choice for the adult coloring enthusiast.

I Love it Coloring Books - An Adult Coloring Book - Cute Owls
By: Clara Hughes - Adult Coloring Books
Copyright Clara Hughes - Images shutterstock.com

ISBN-13: 978-1532770111

ISBN-10: 1532770111

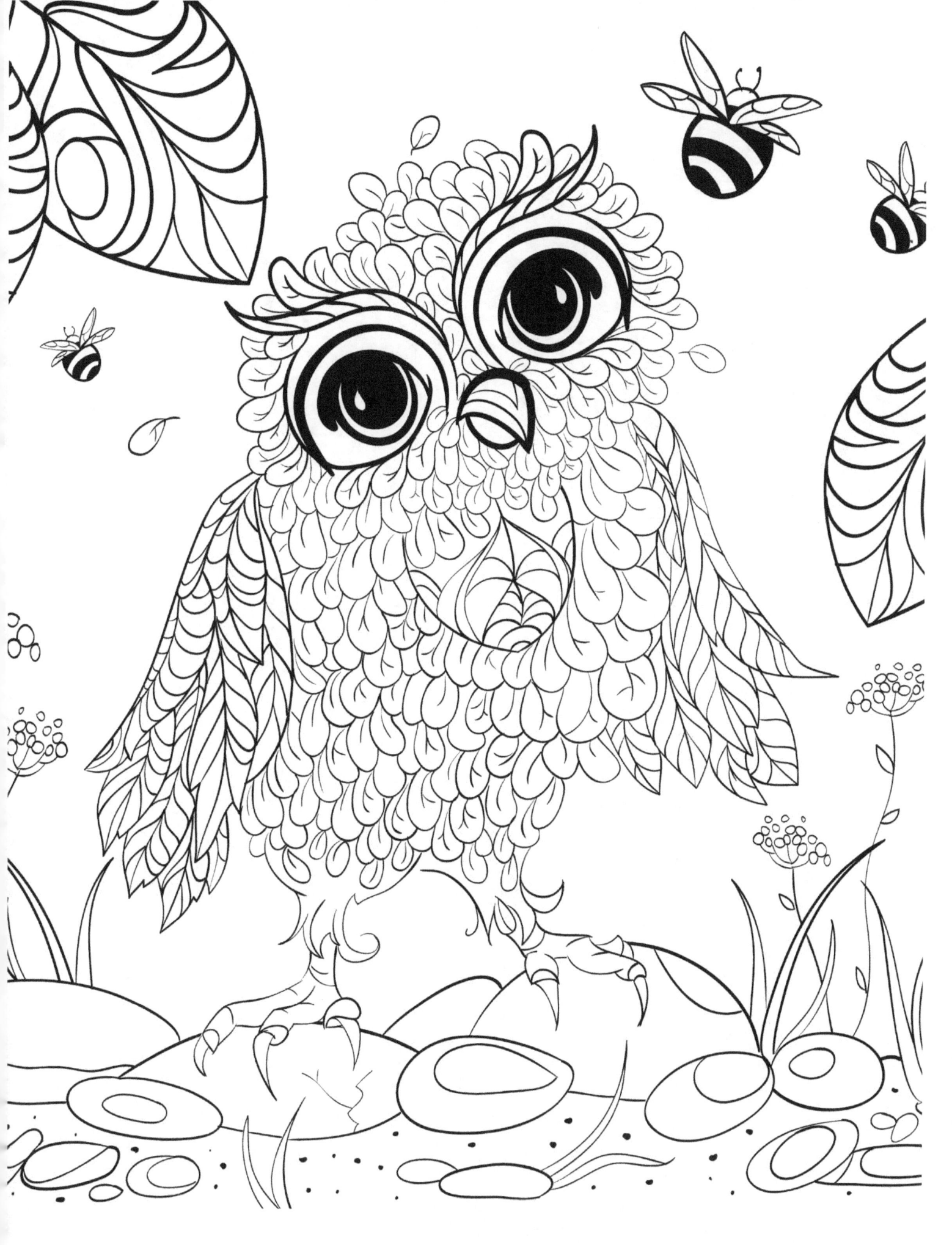

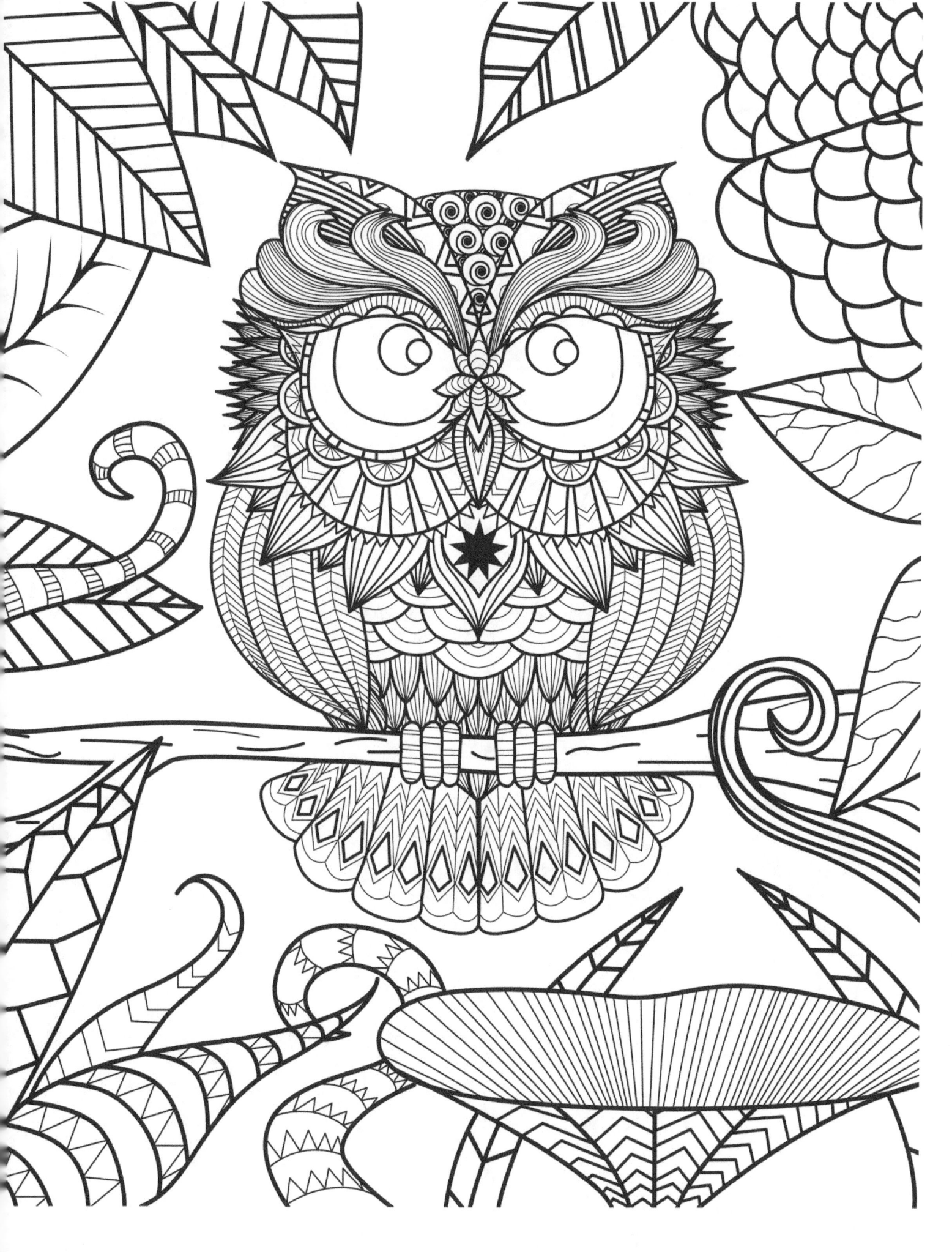

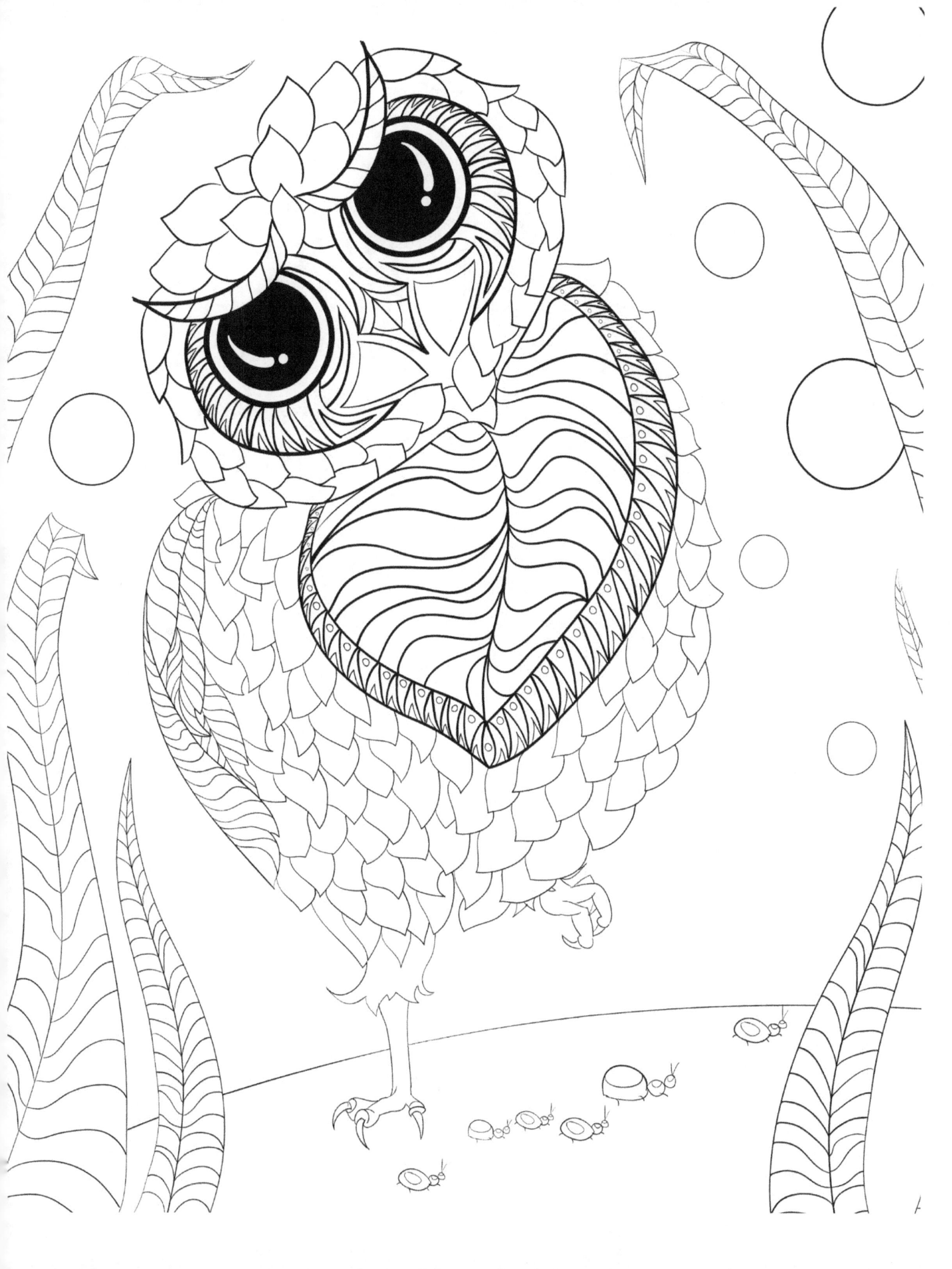

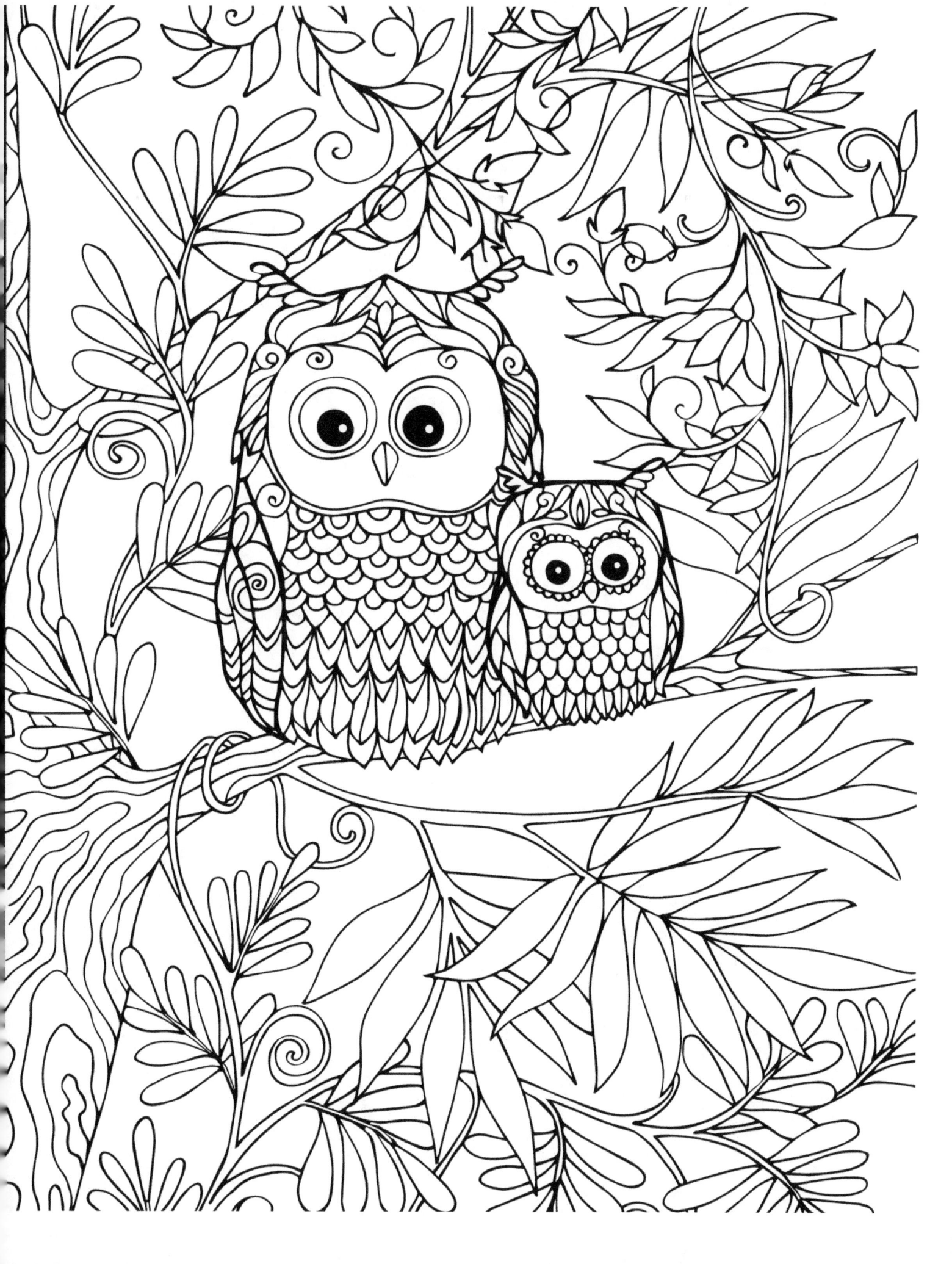

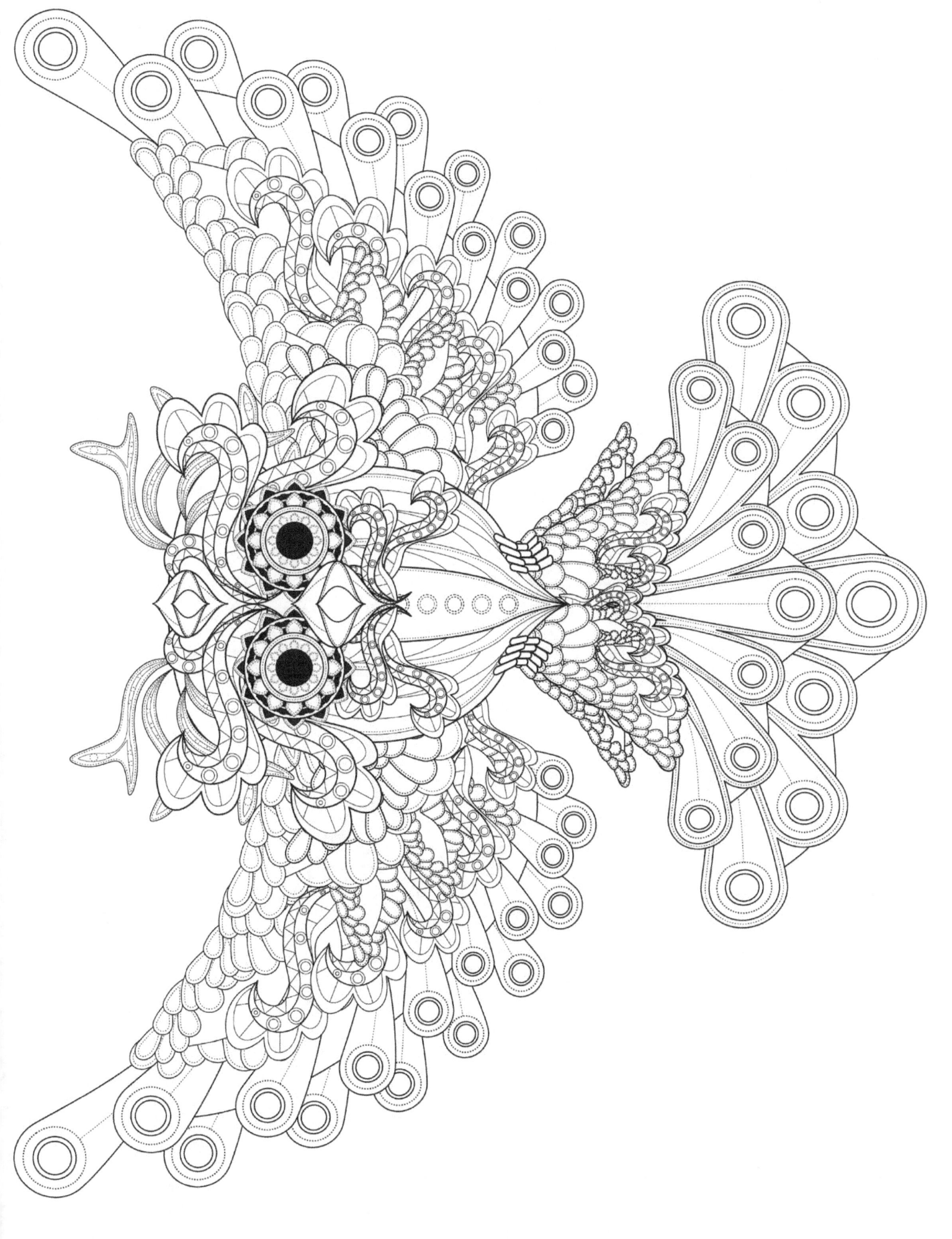

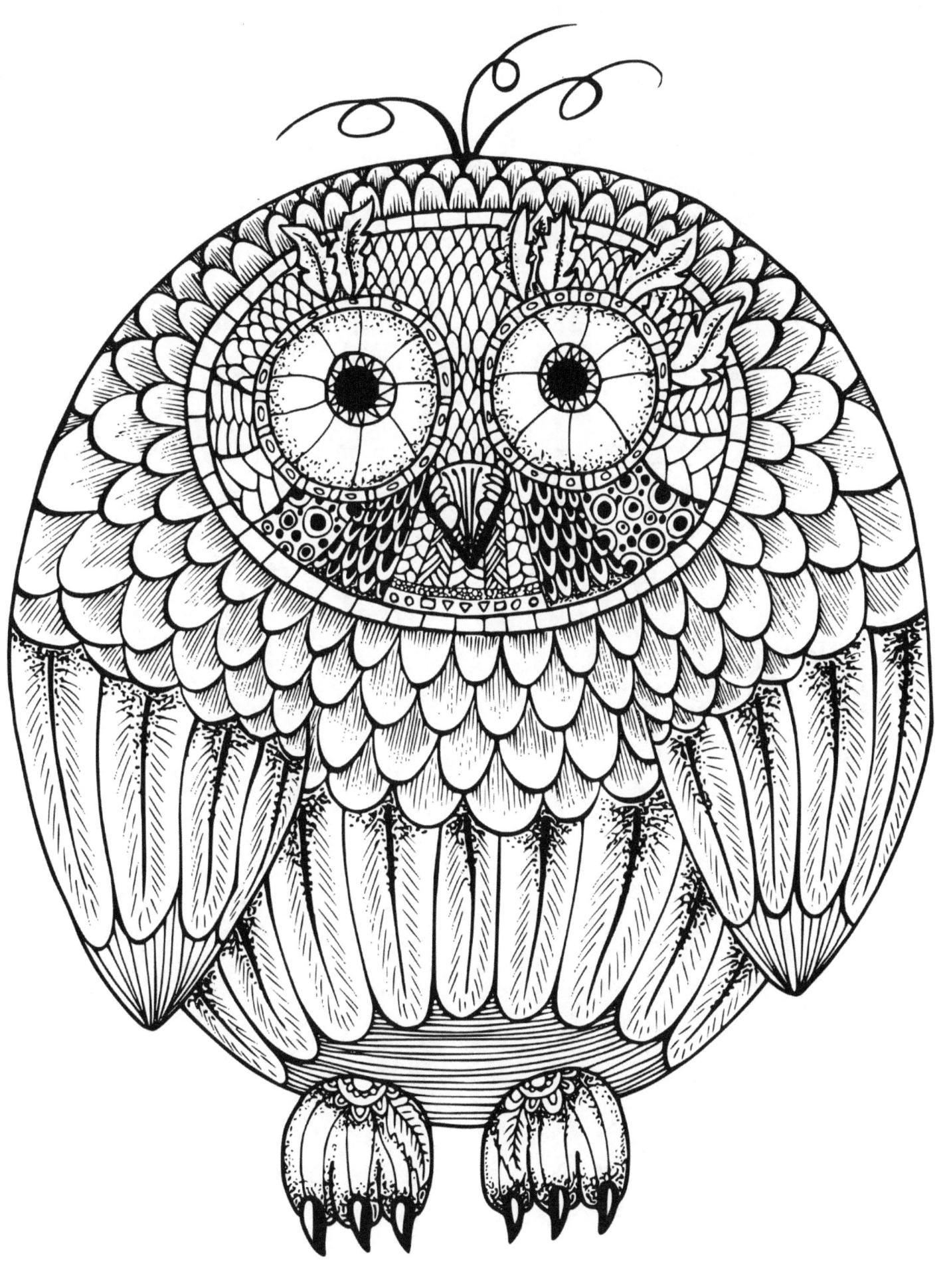

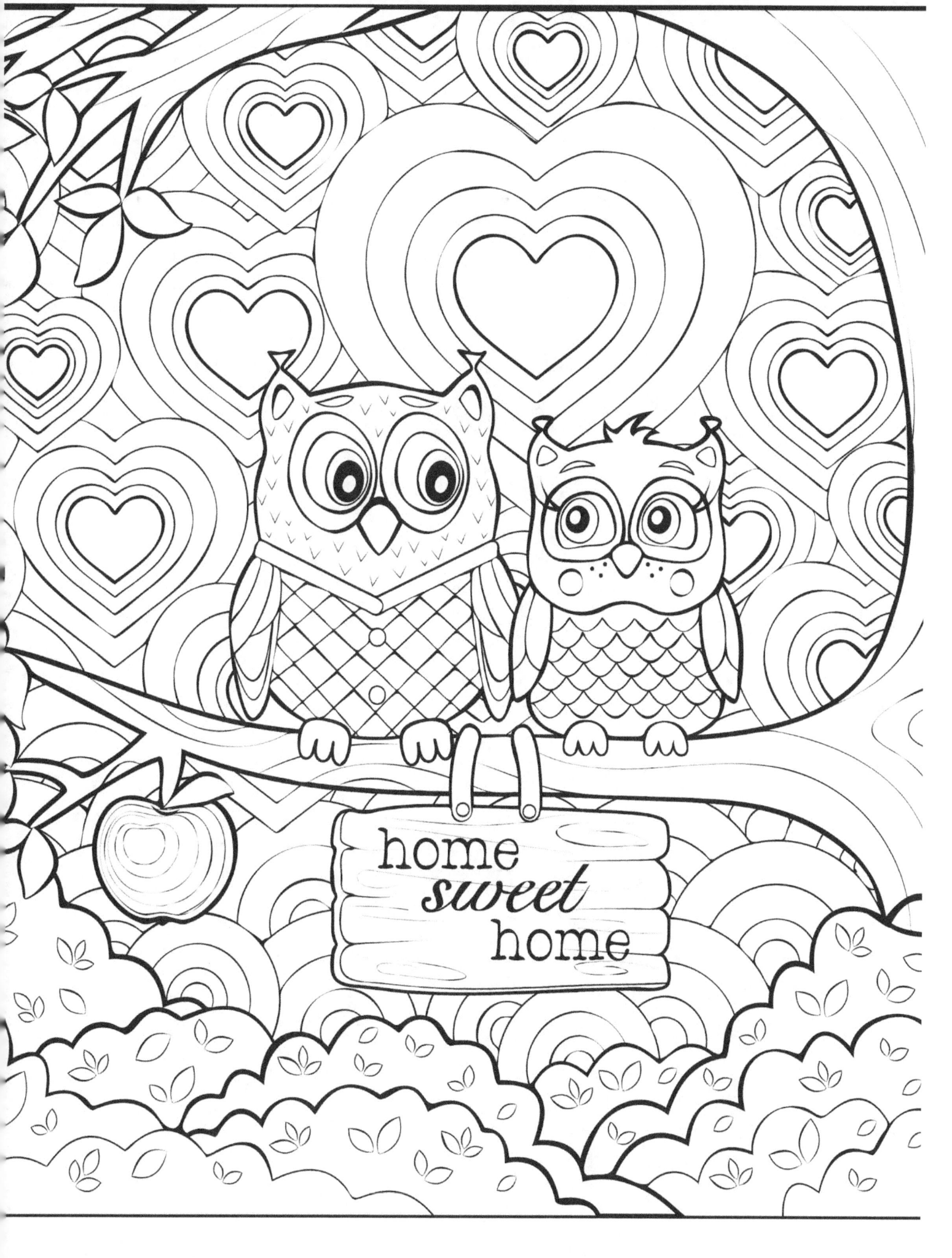

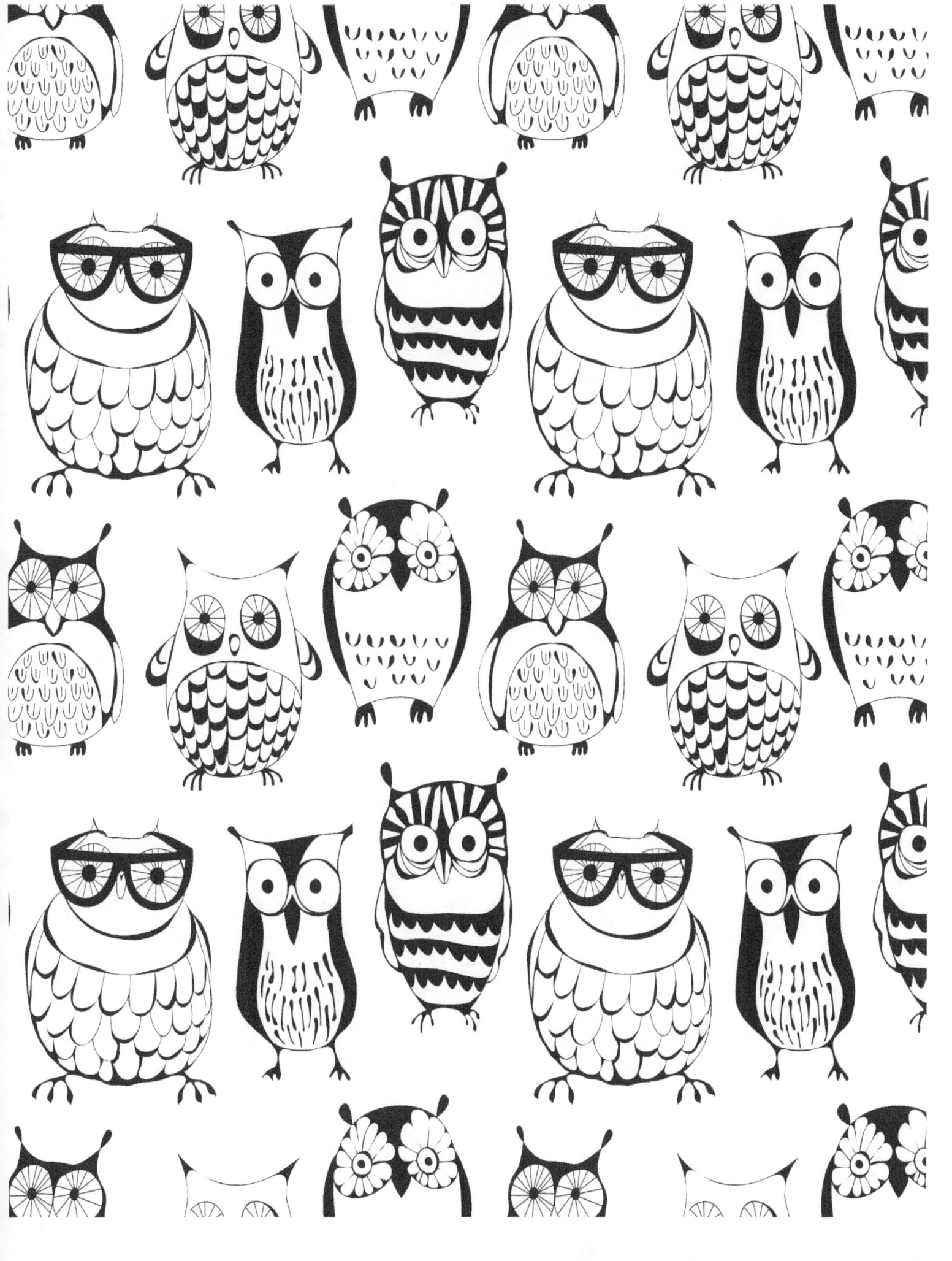

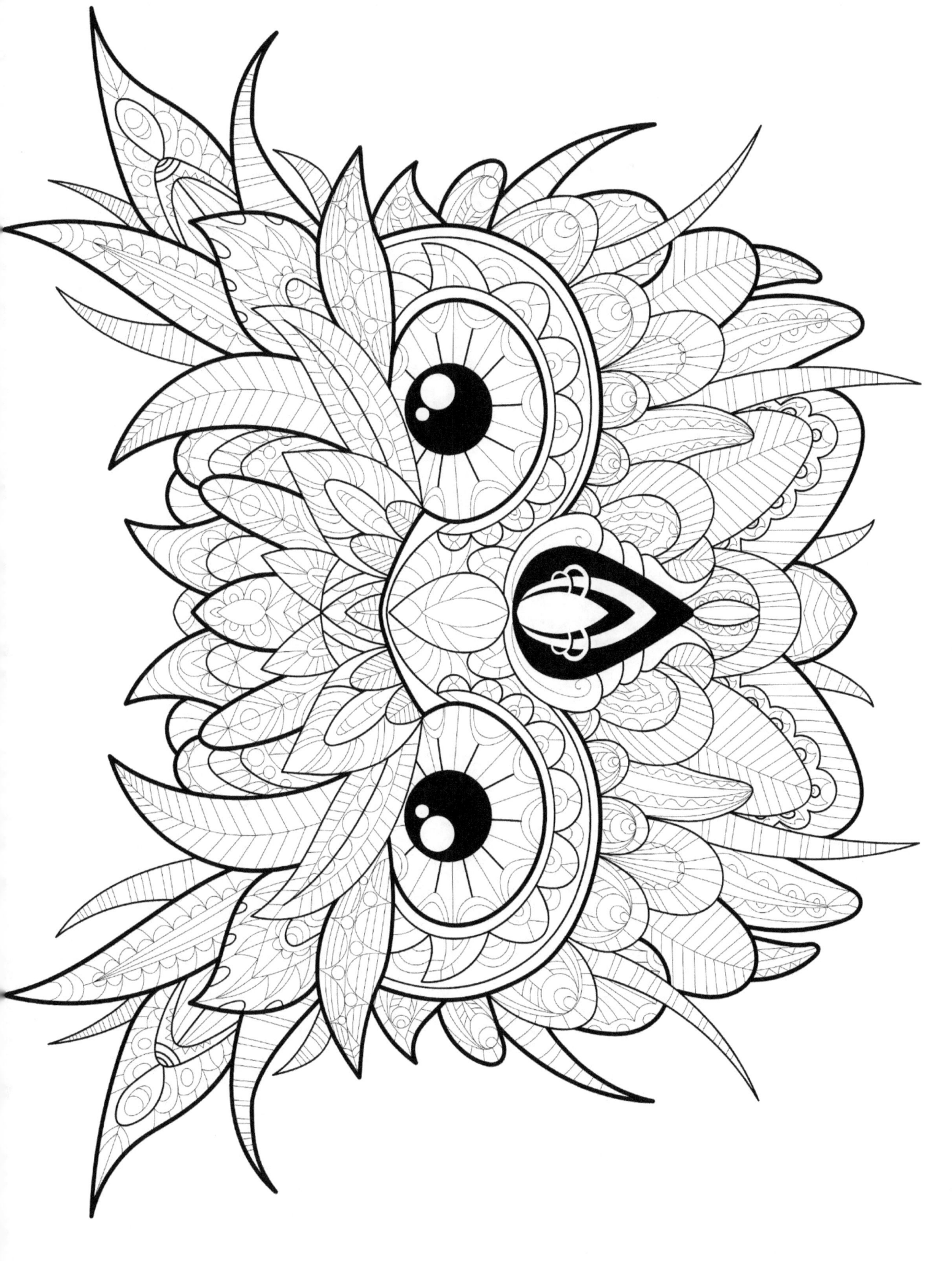

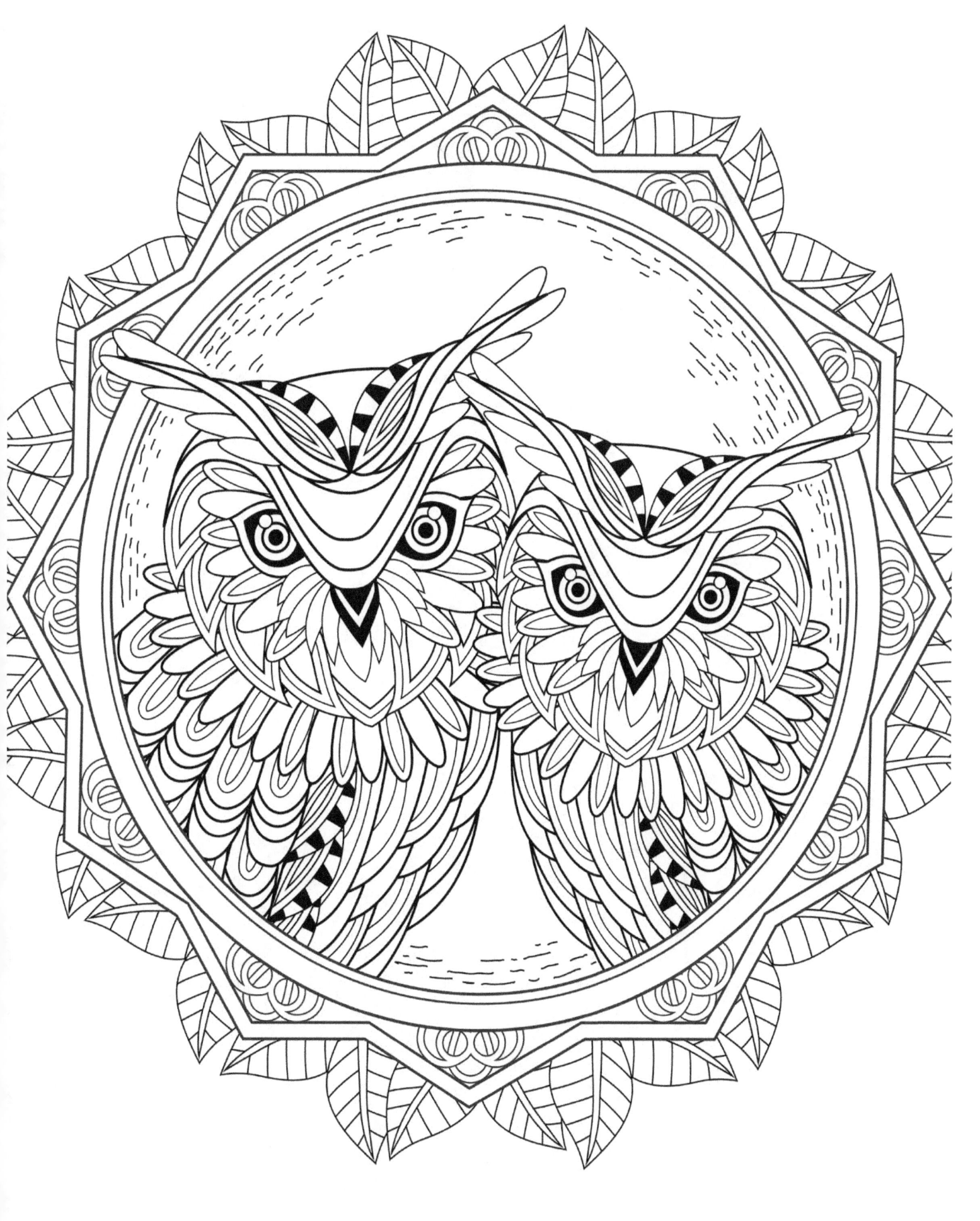

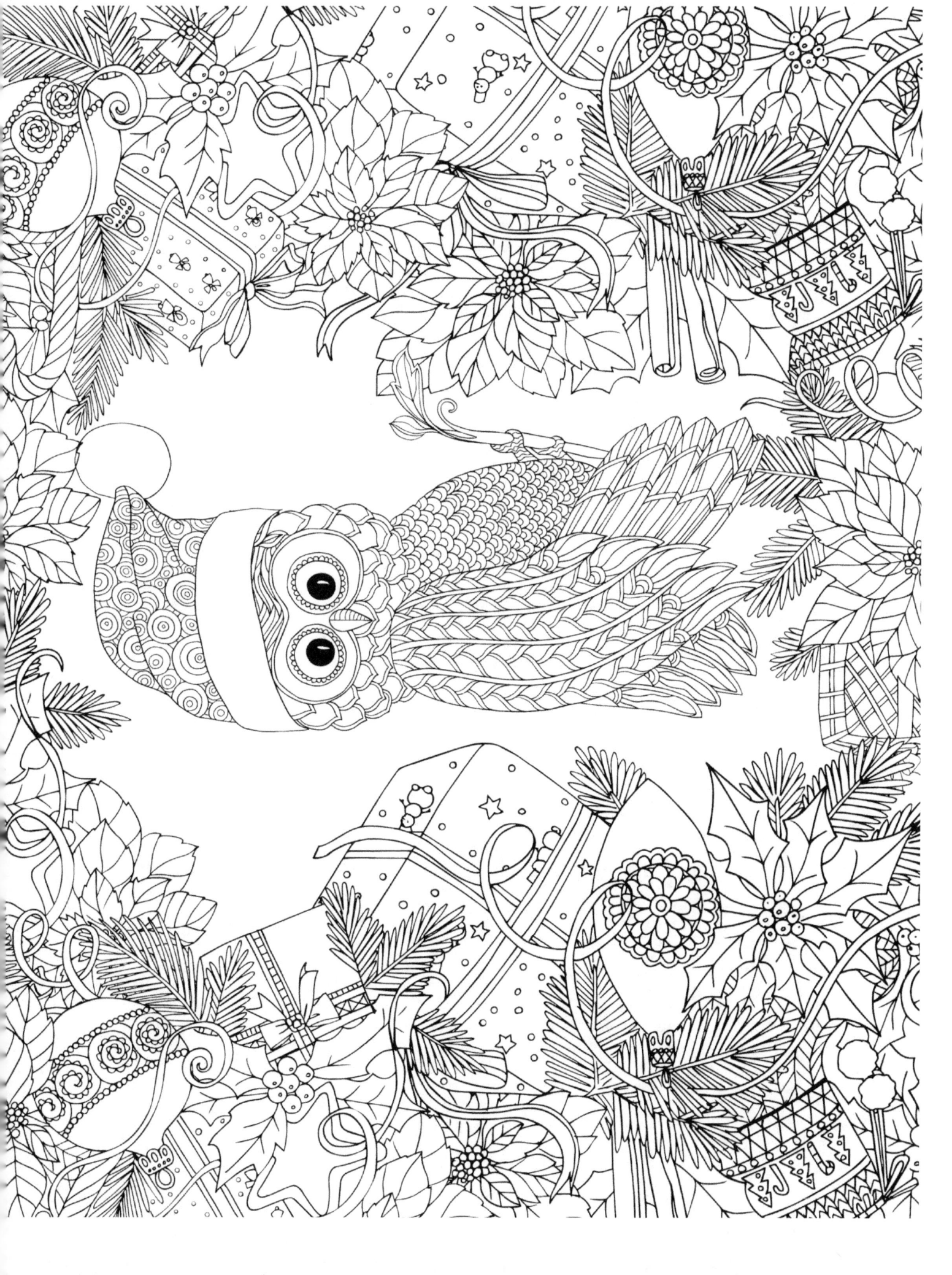

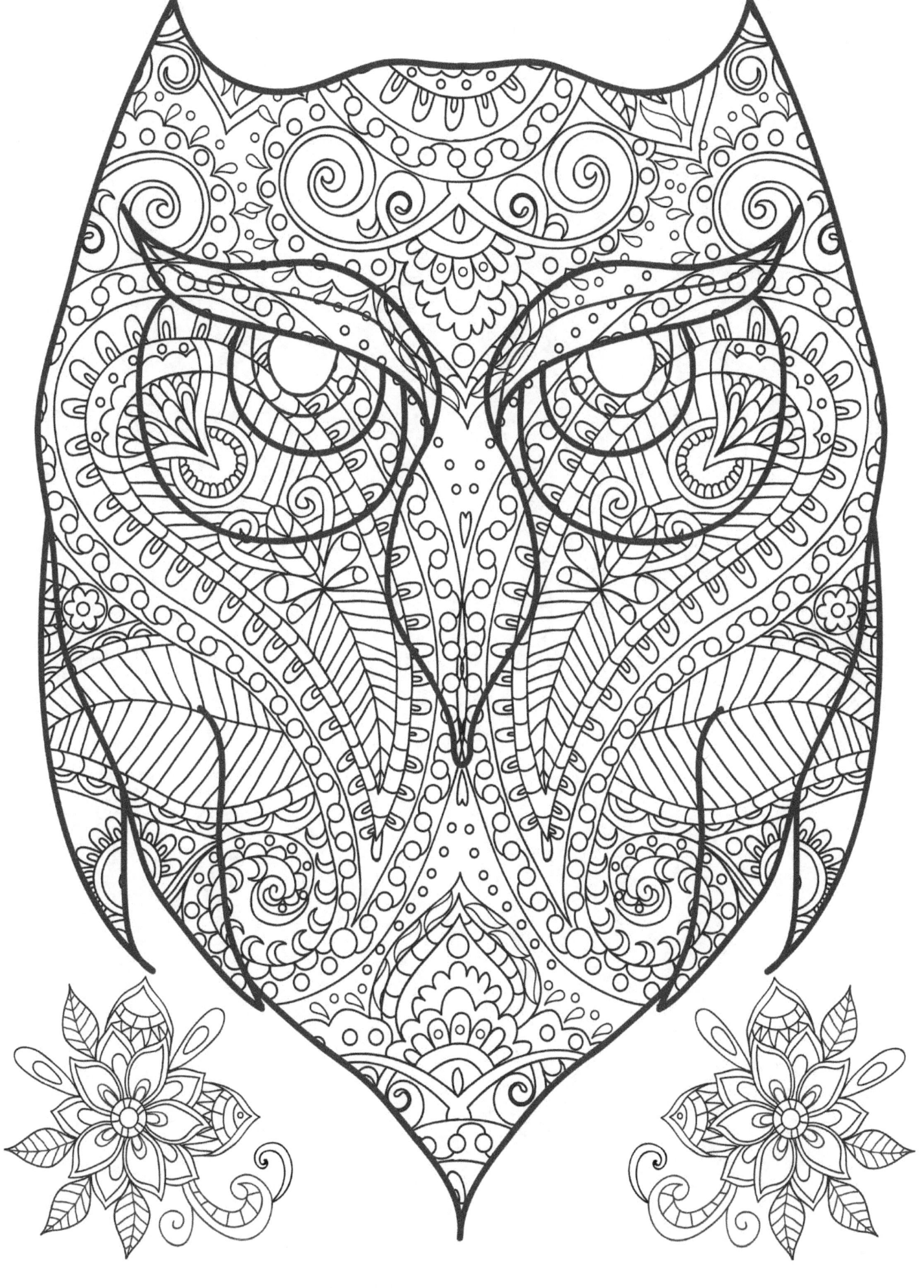

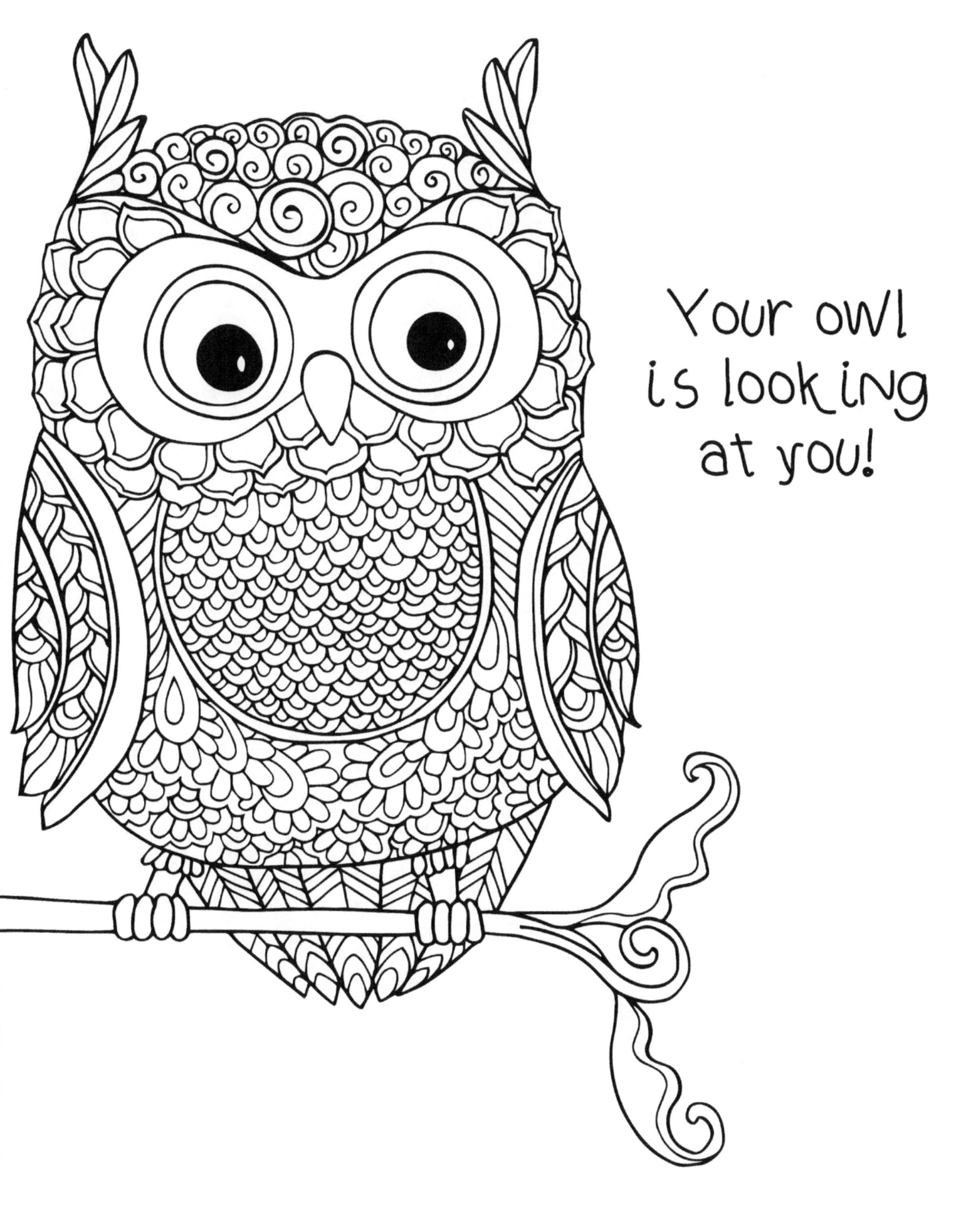

Your owl is looking at you!

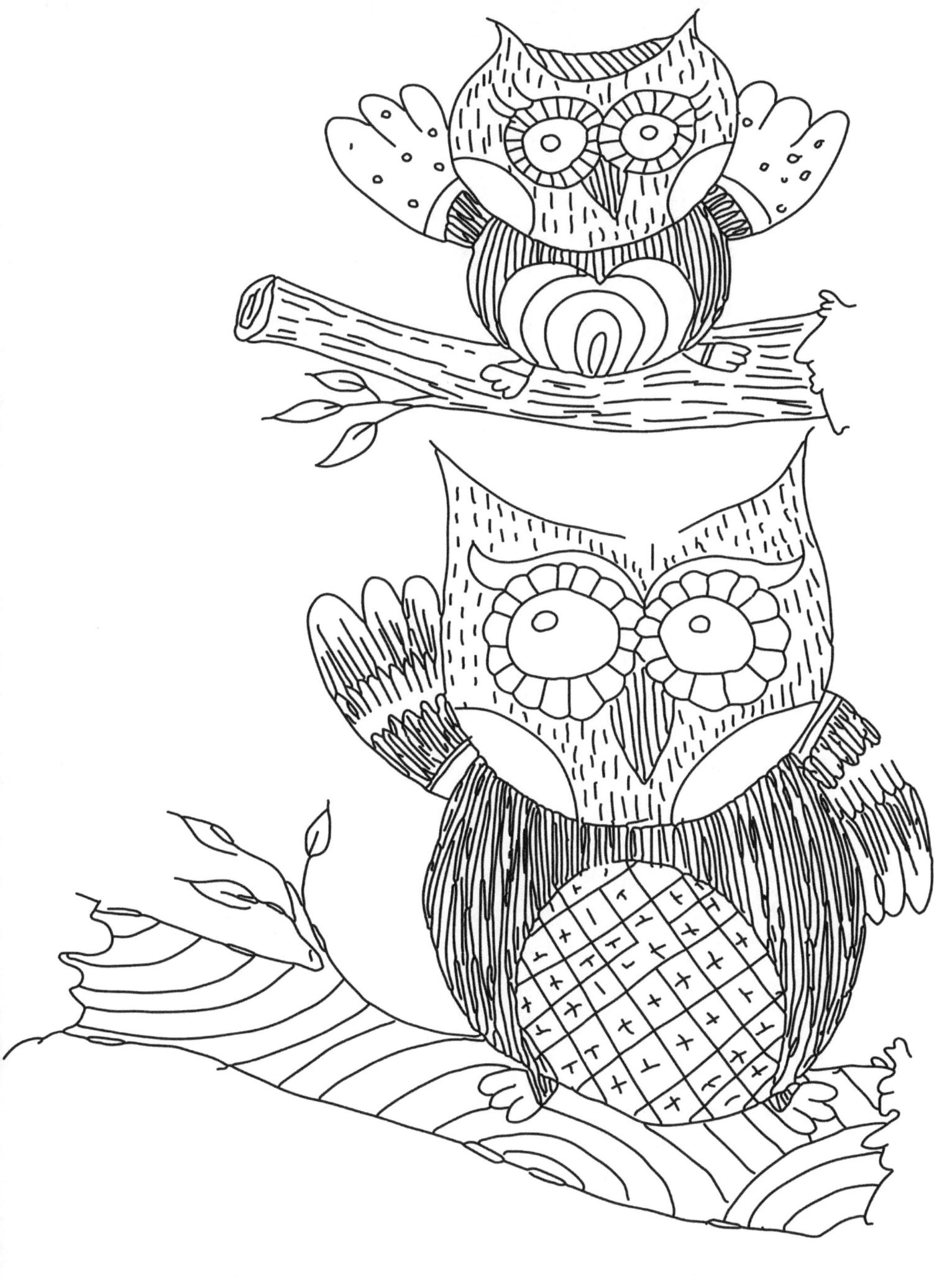

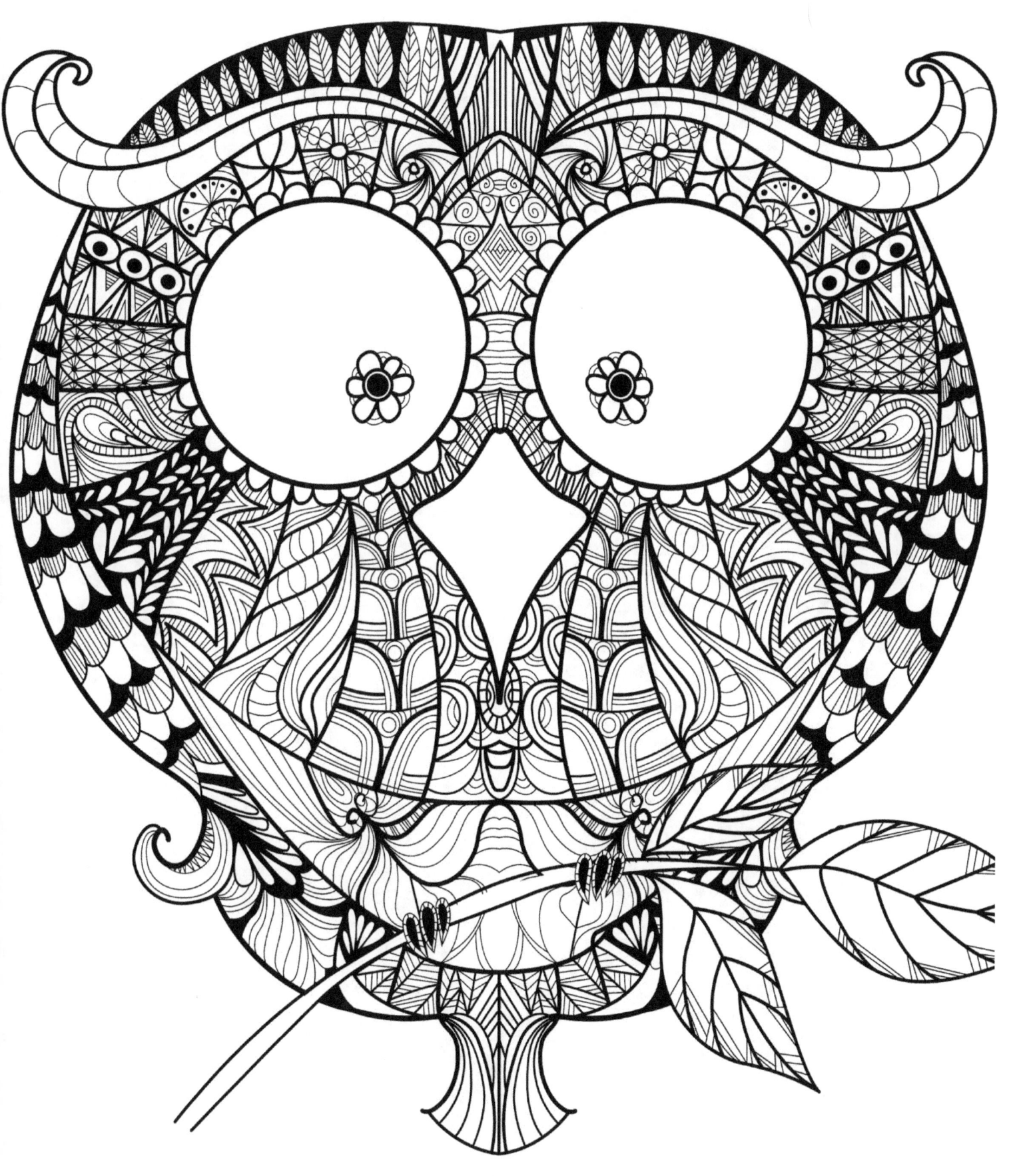

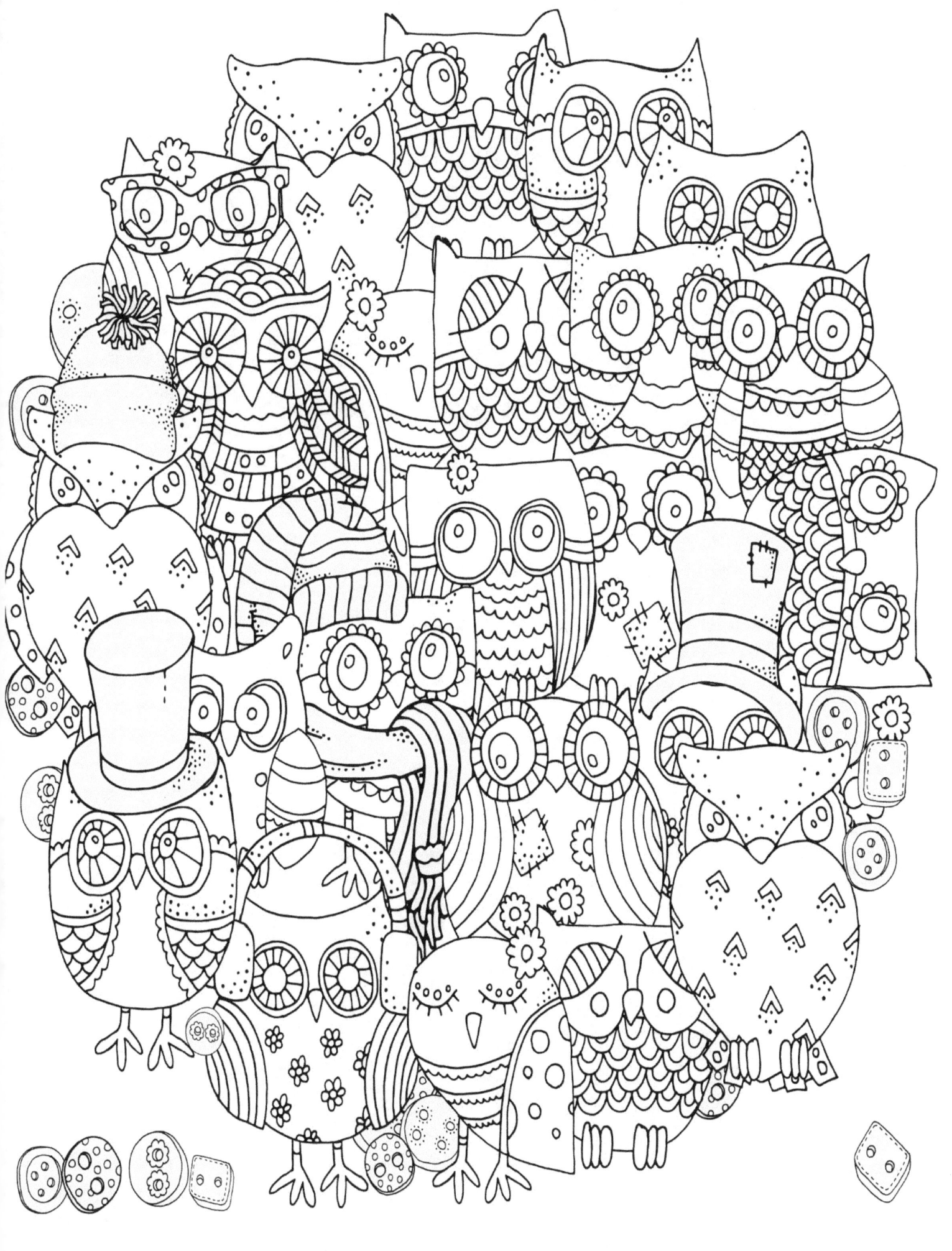

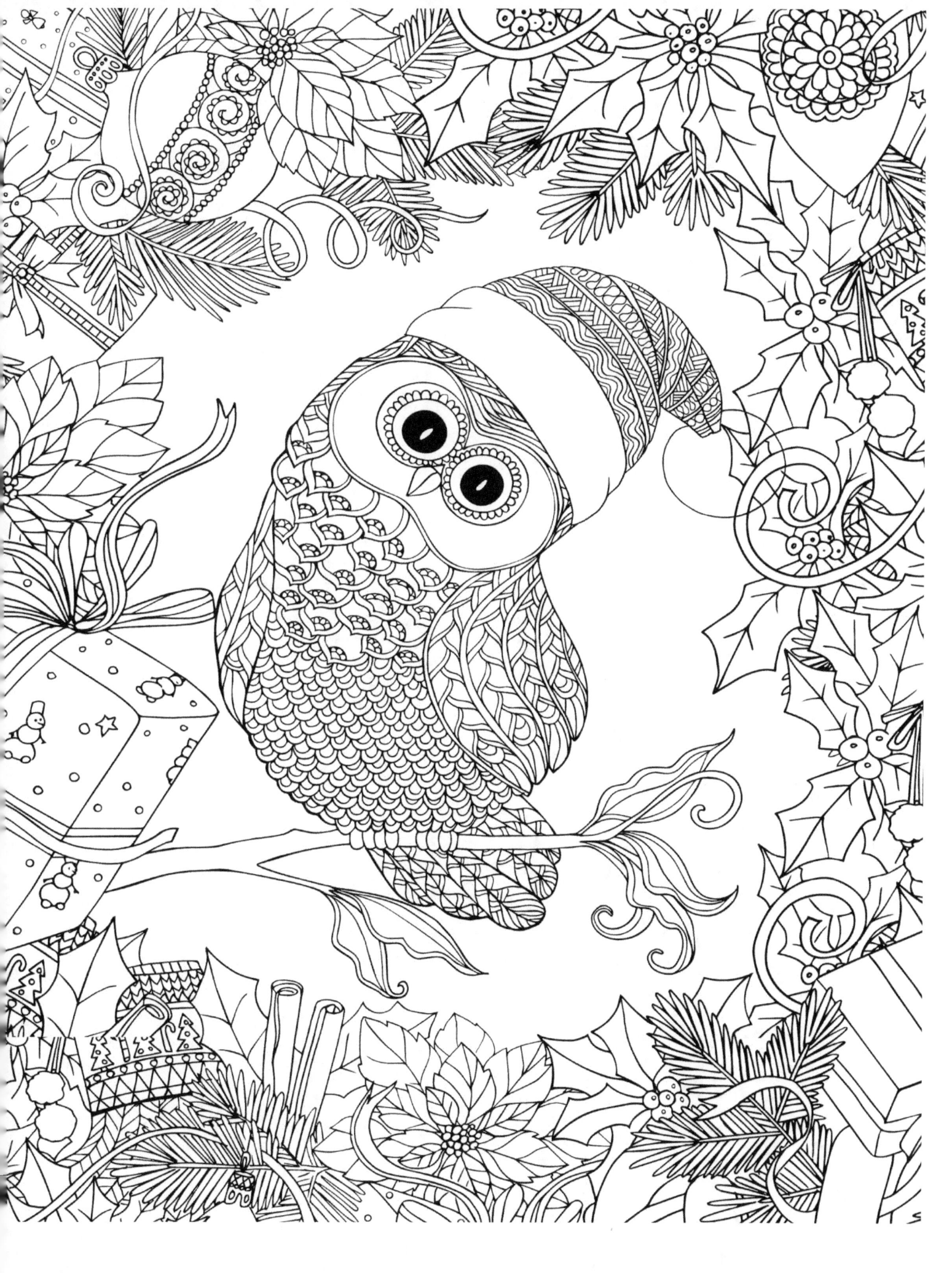

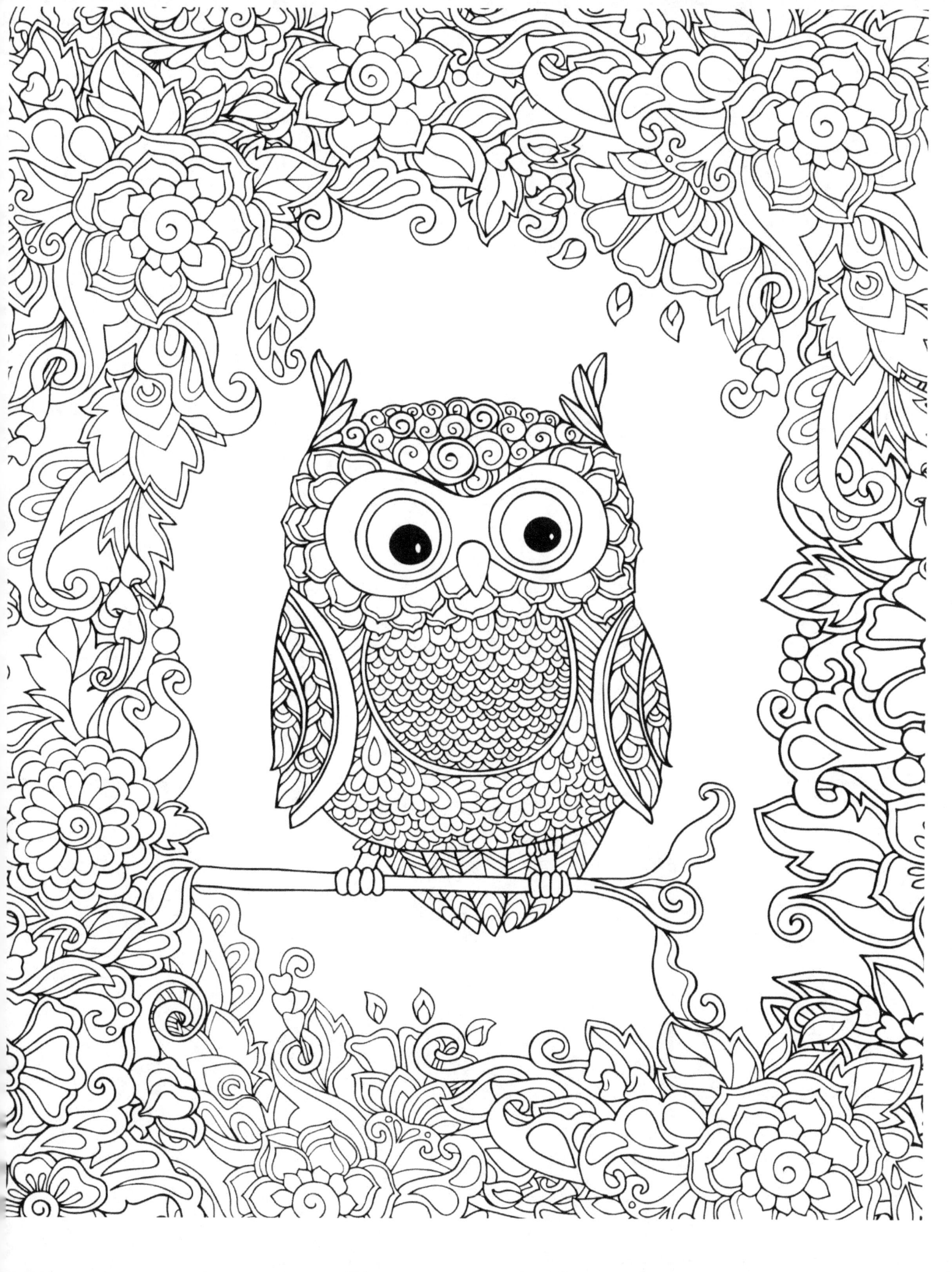

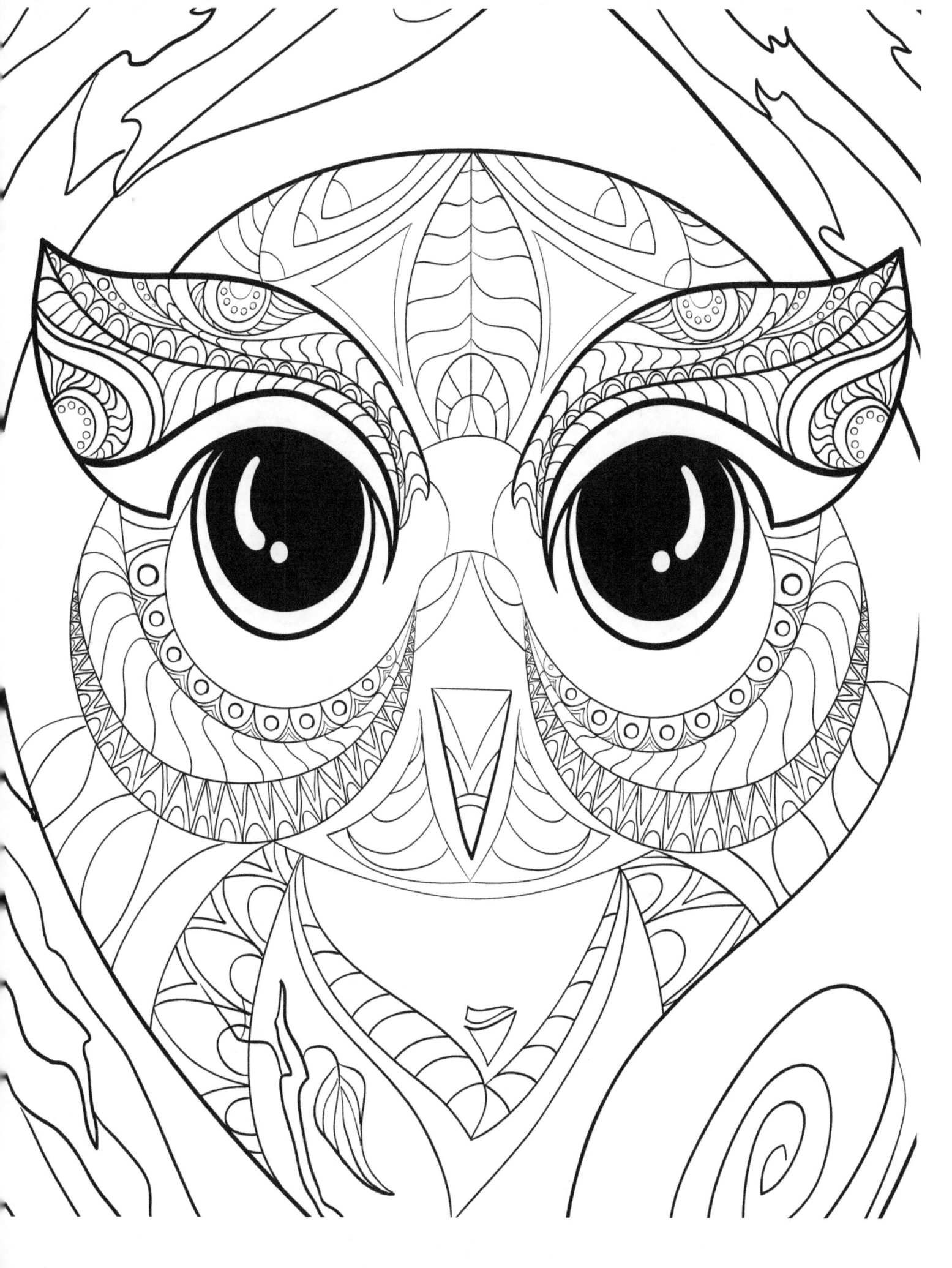

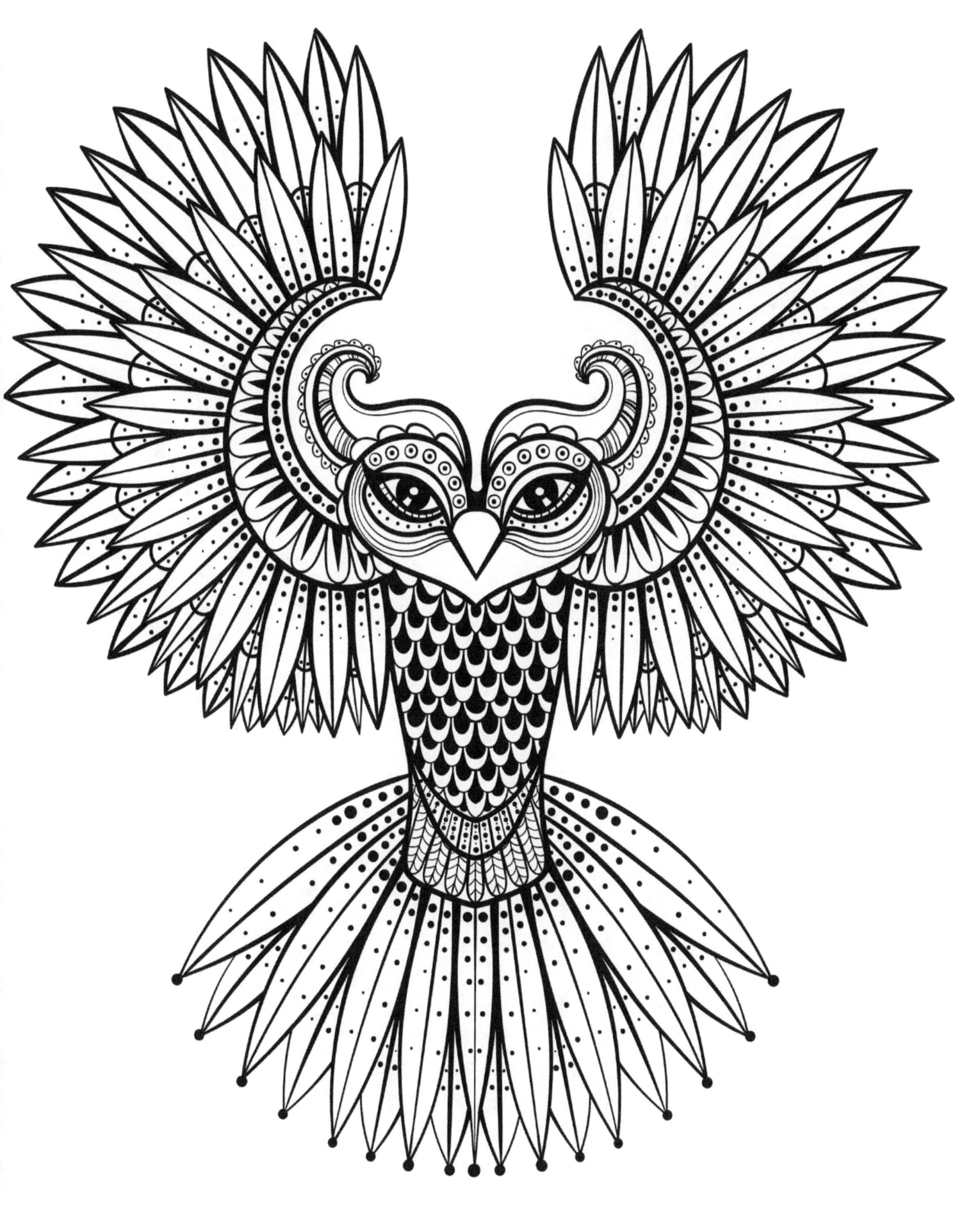

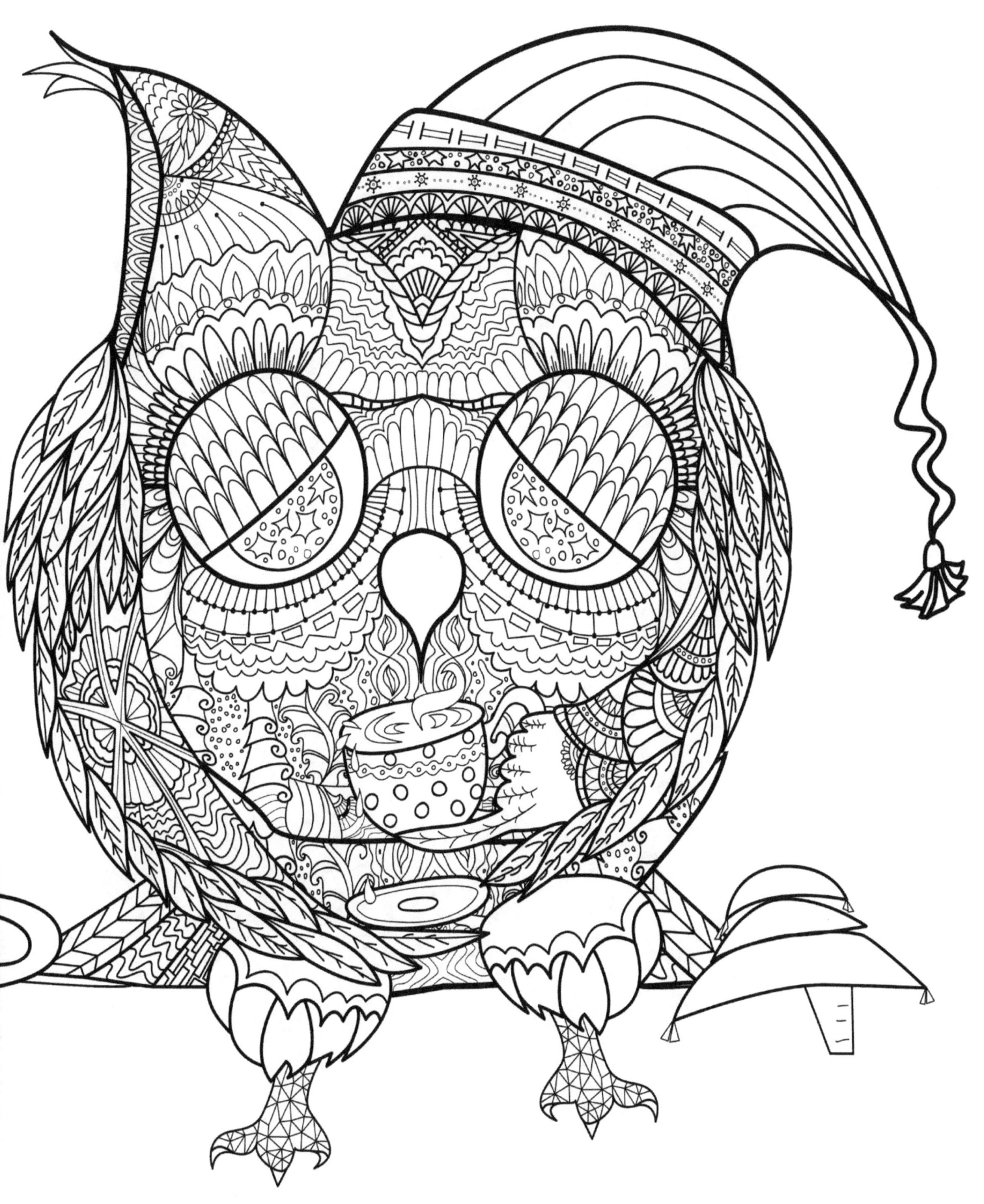

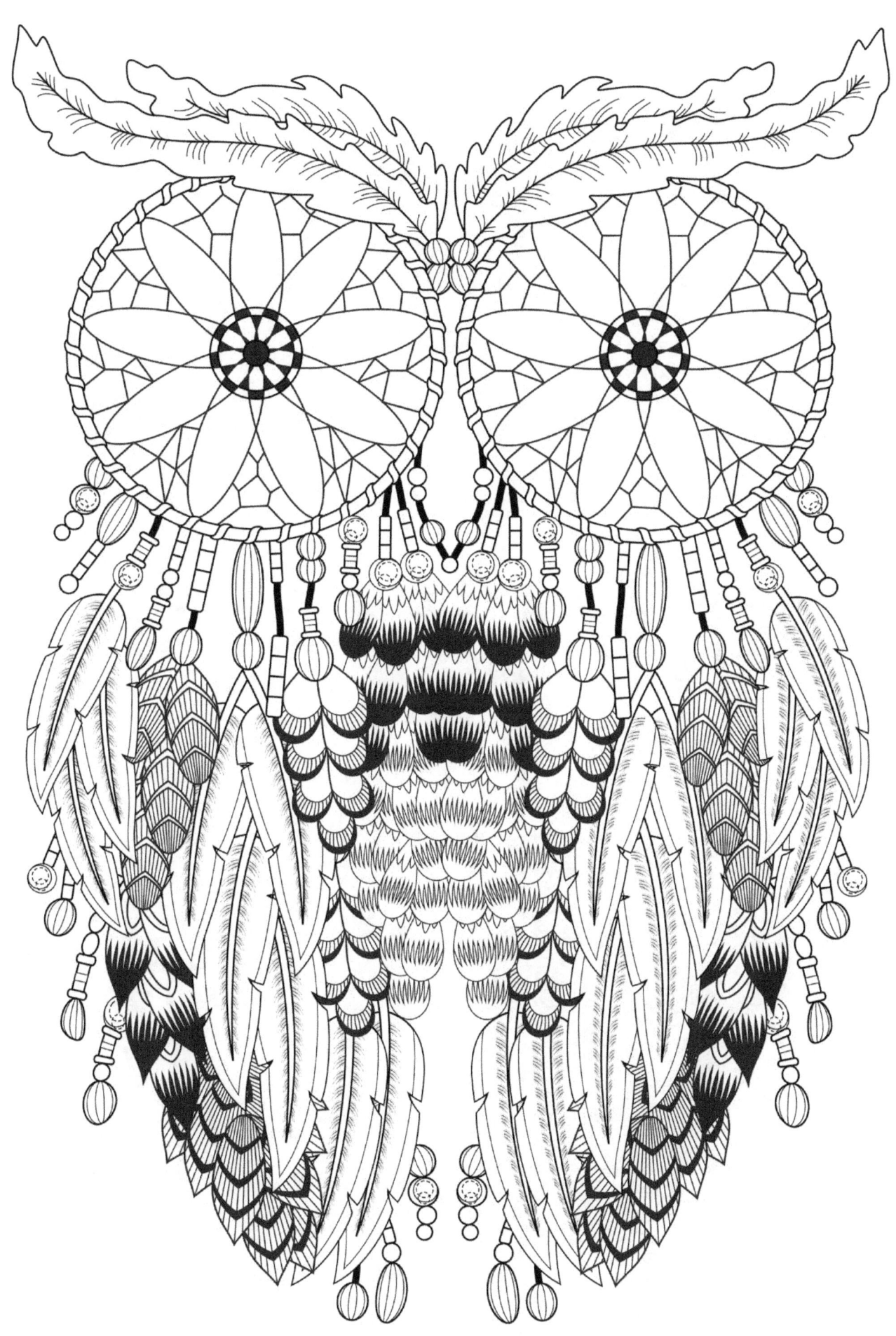

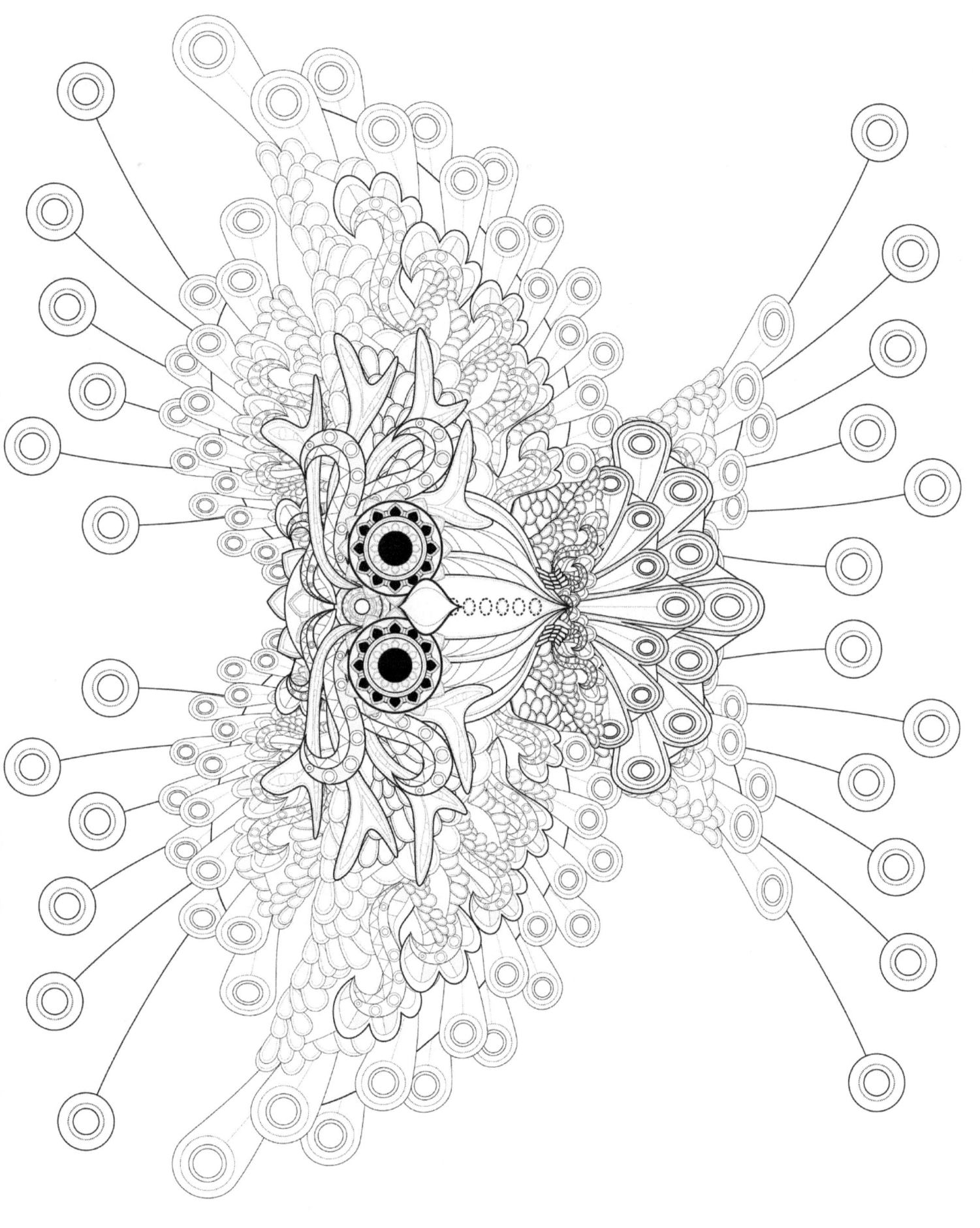

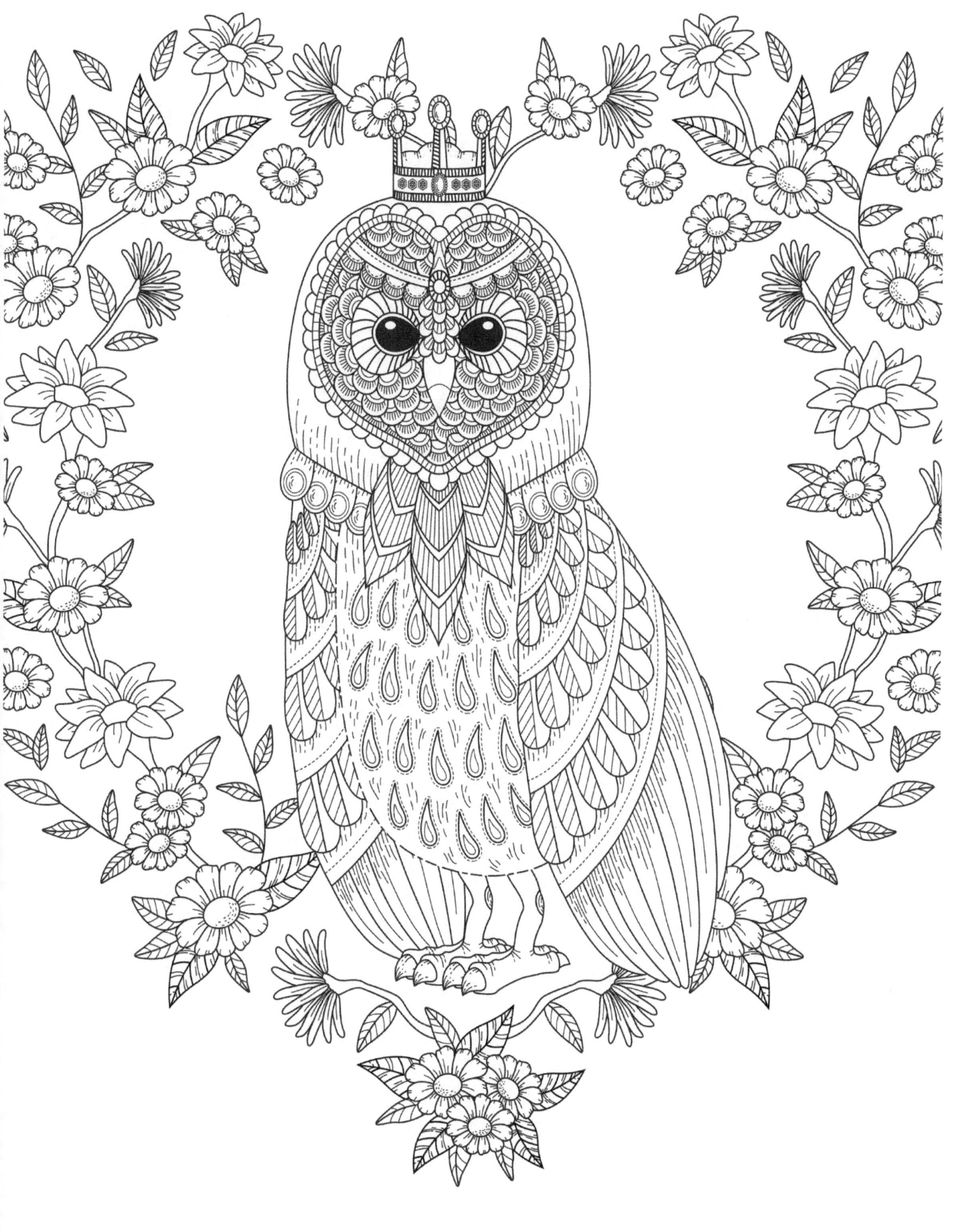

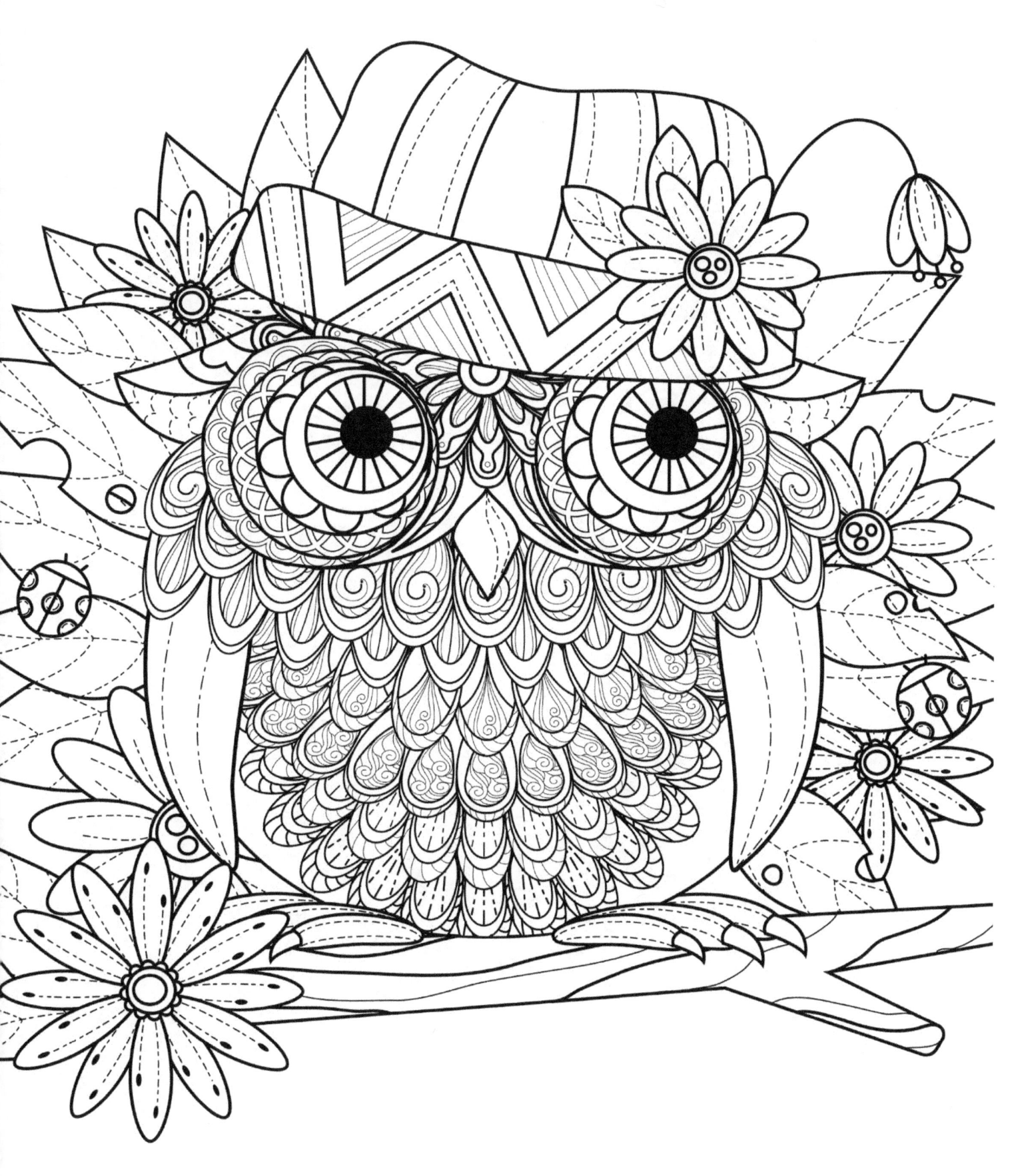

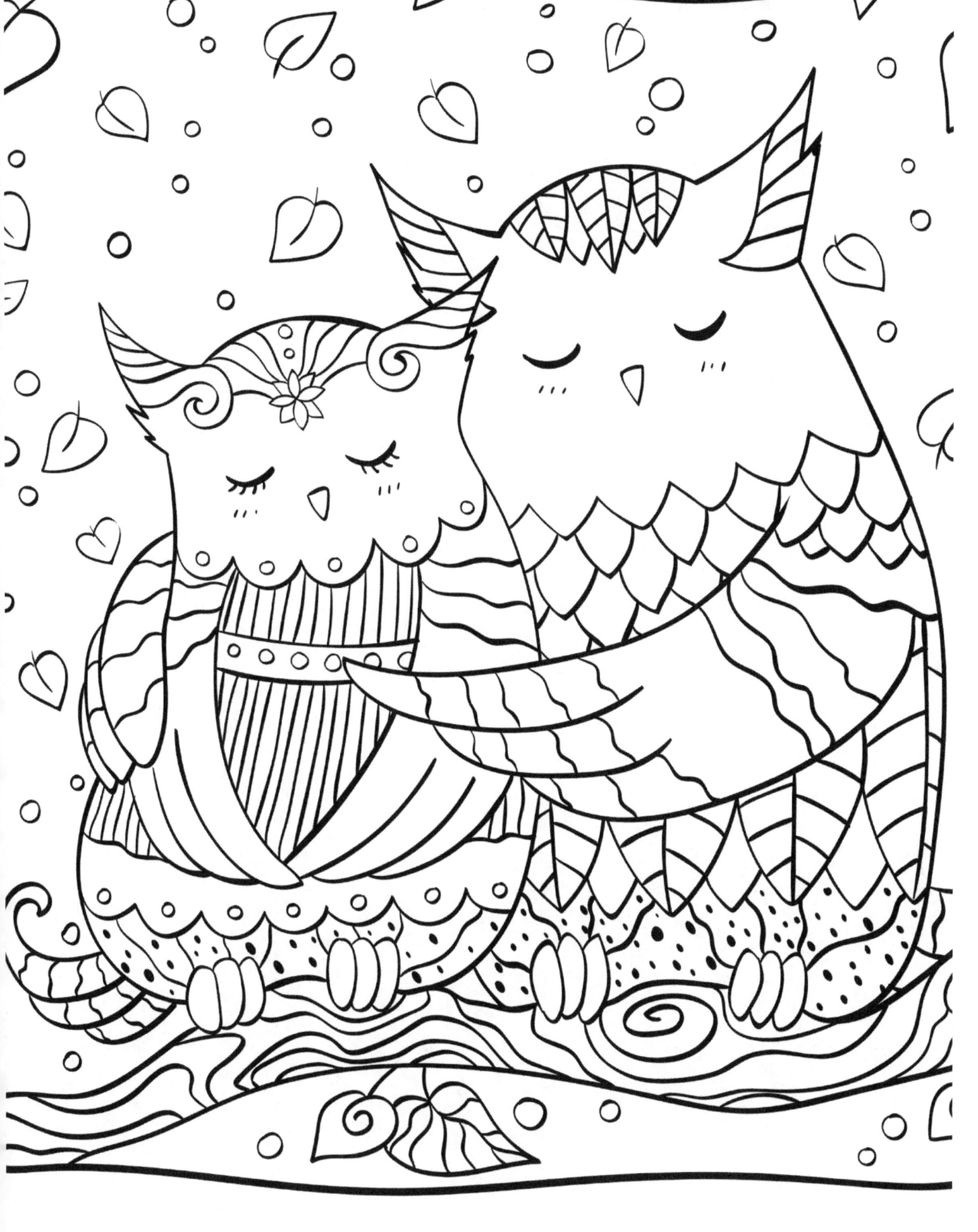

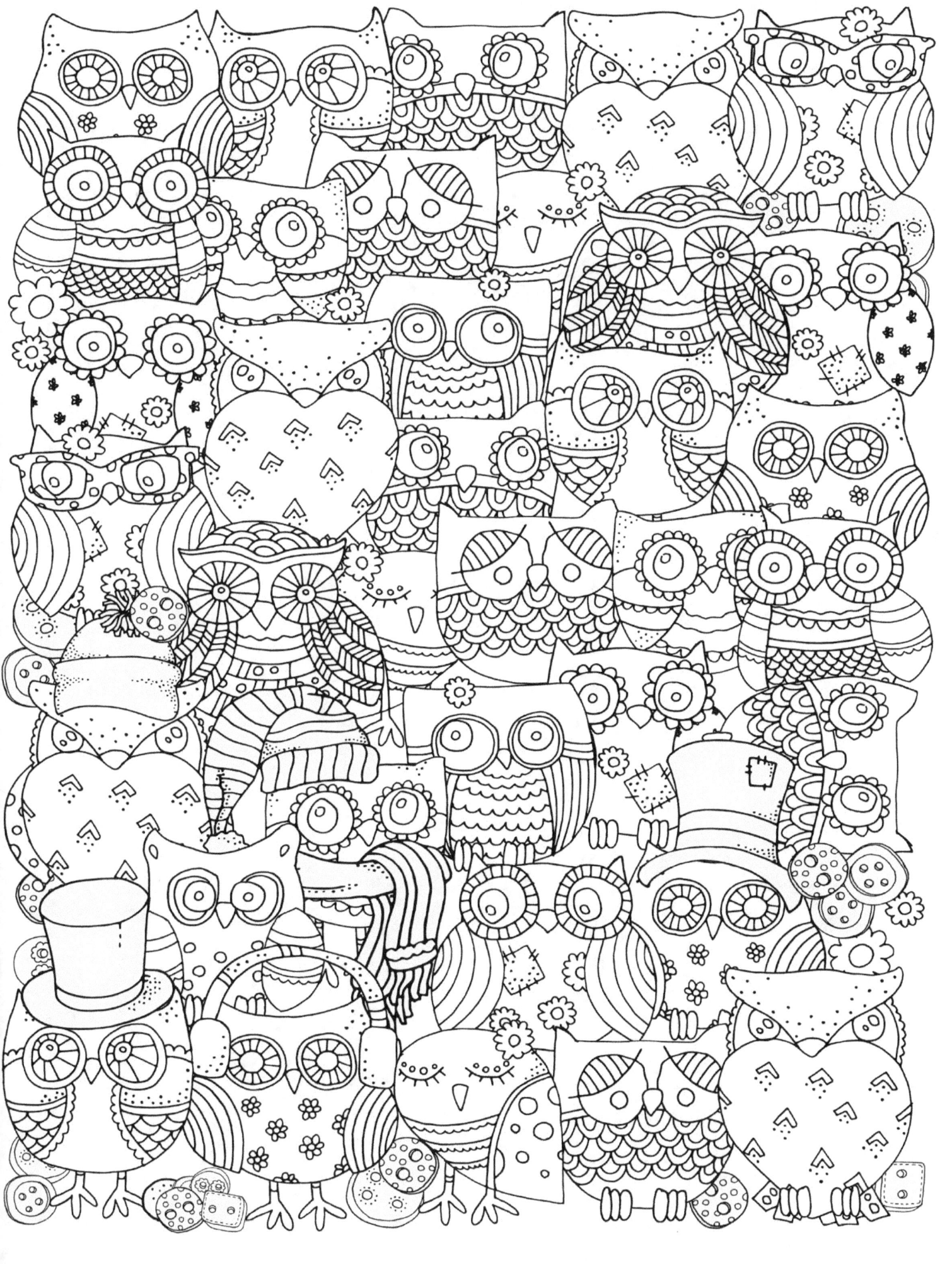

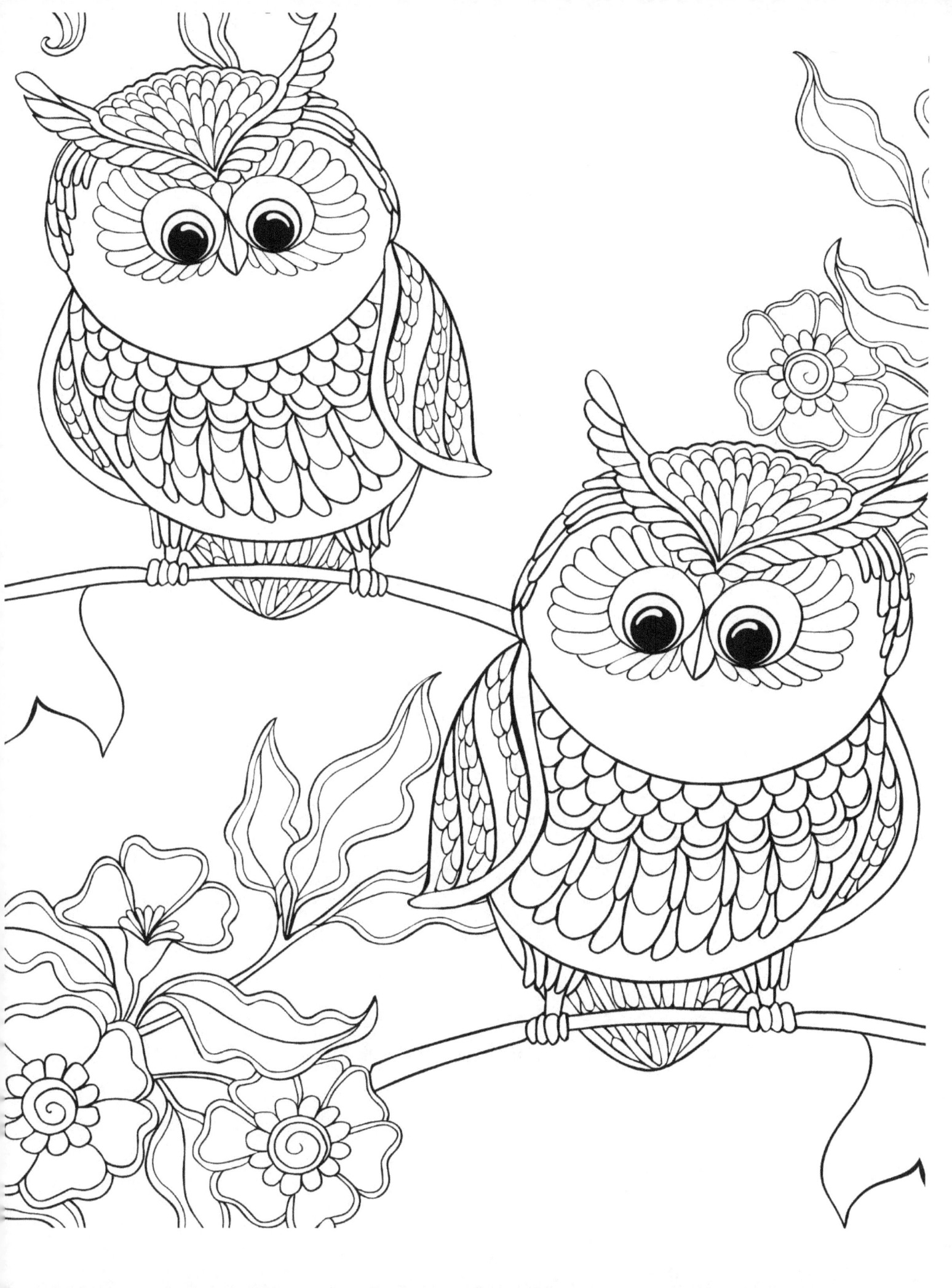

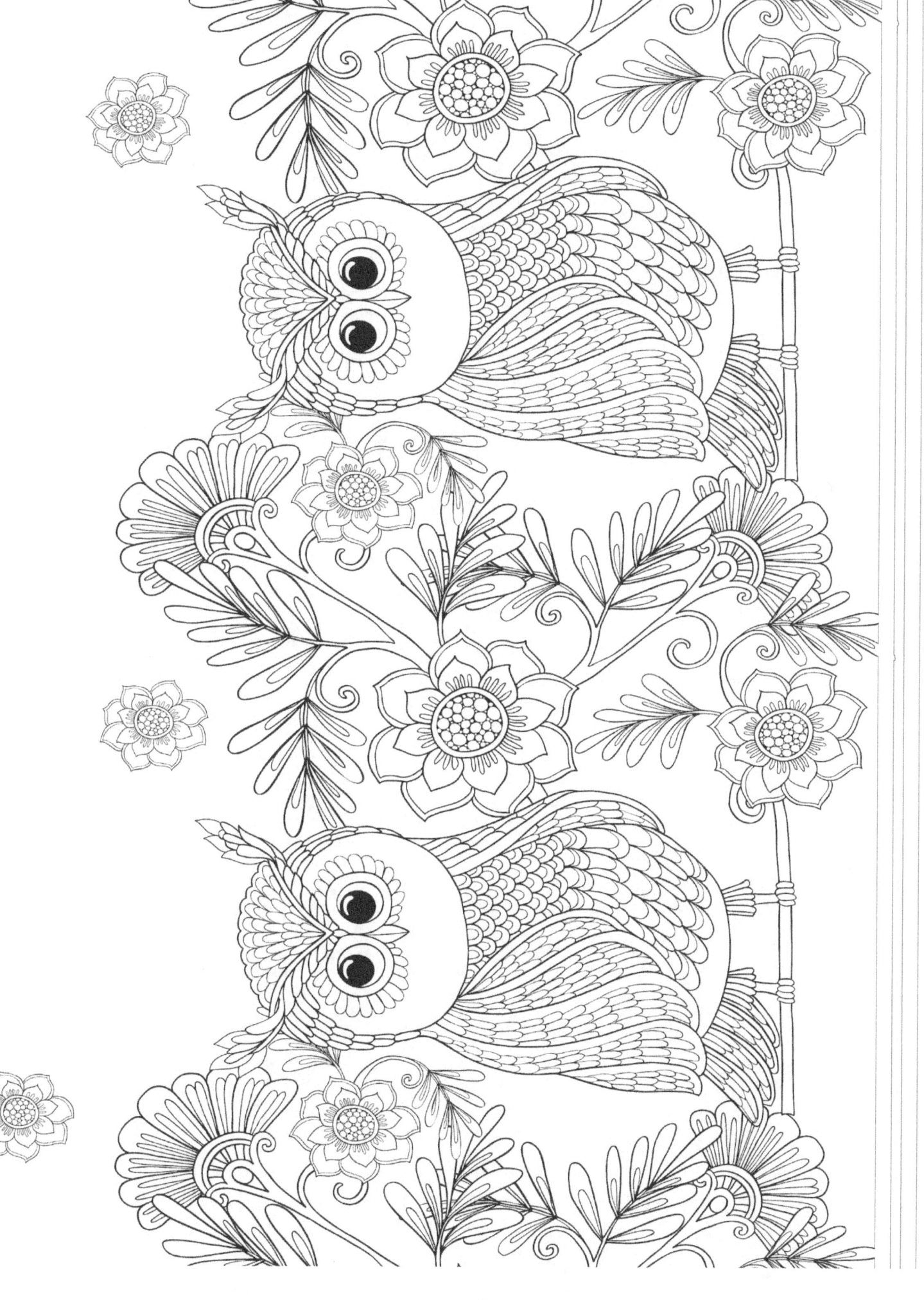

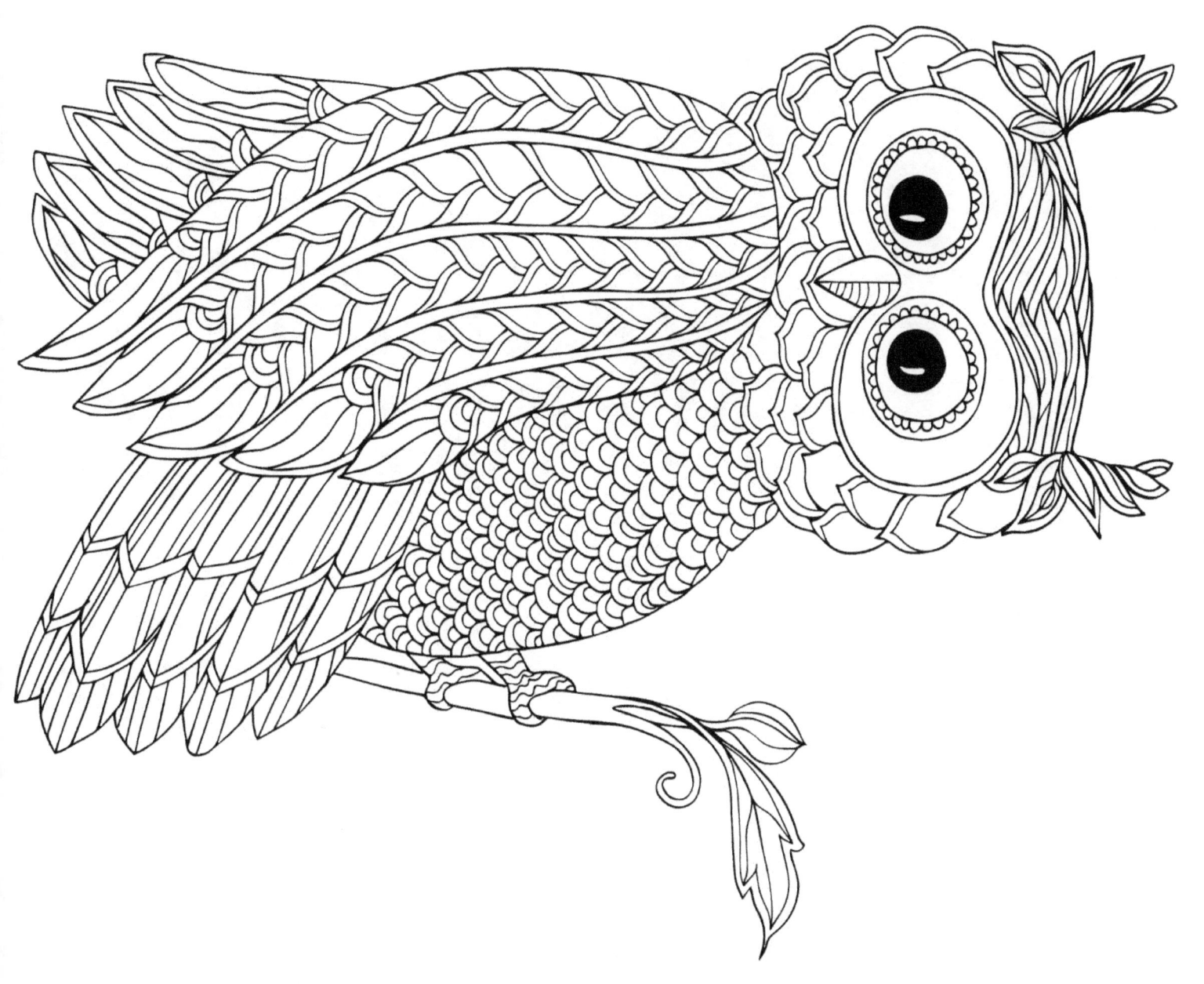

Your owl
is looking
at you!

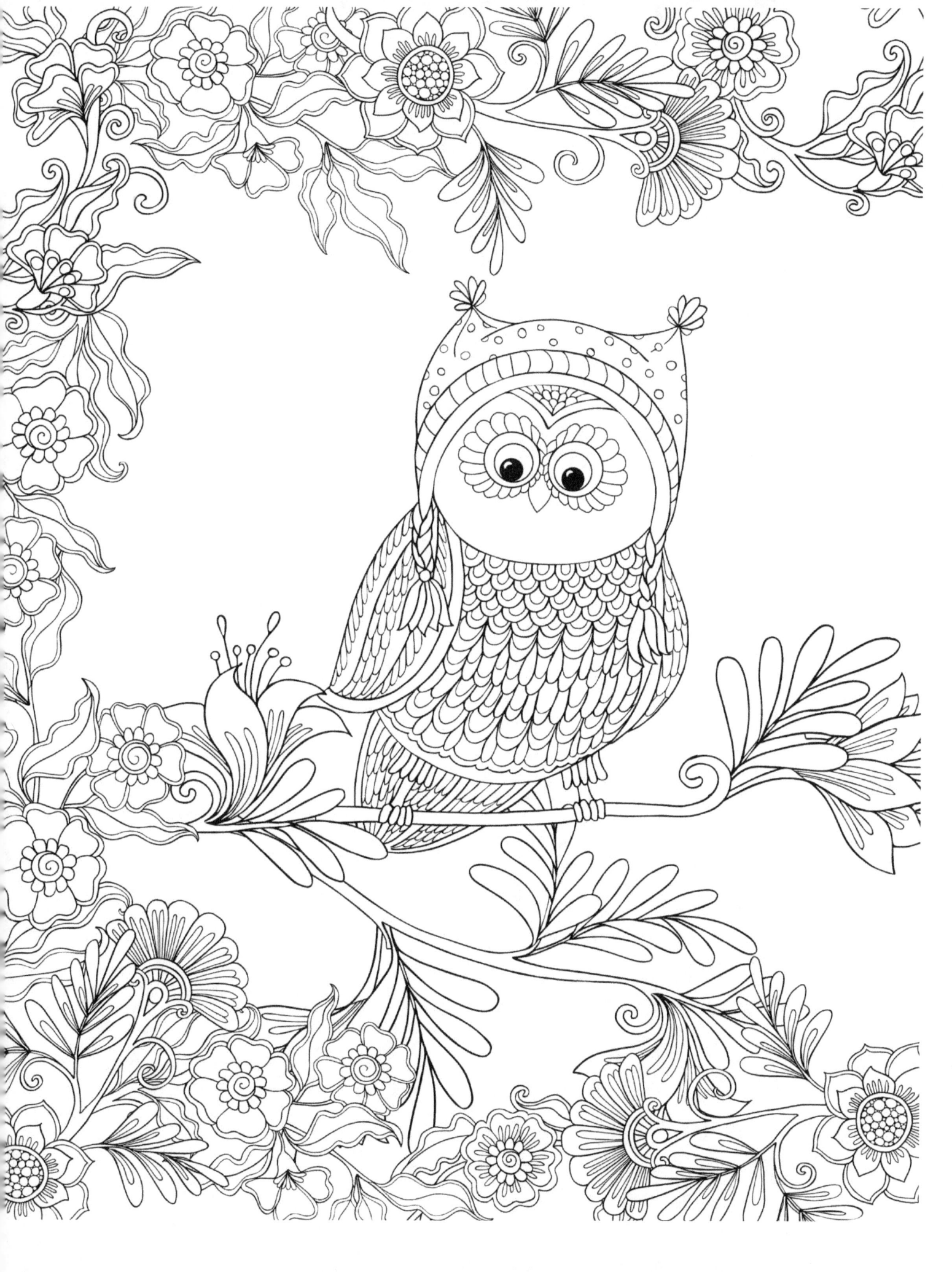

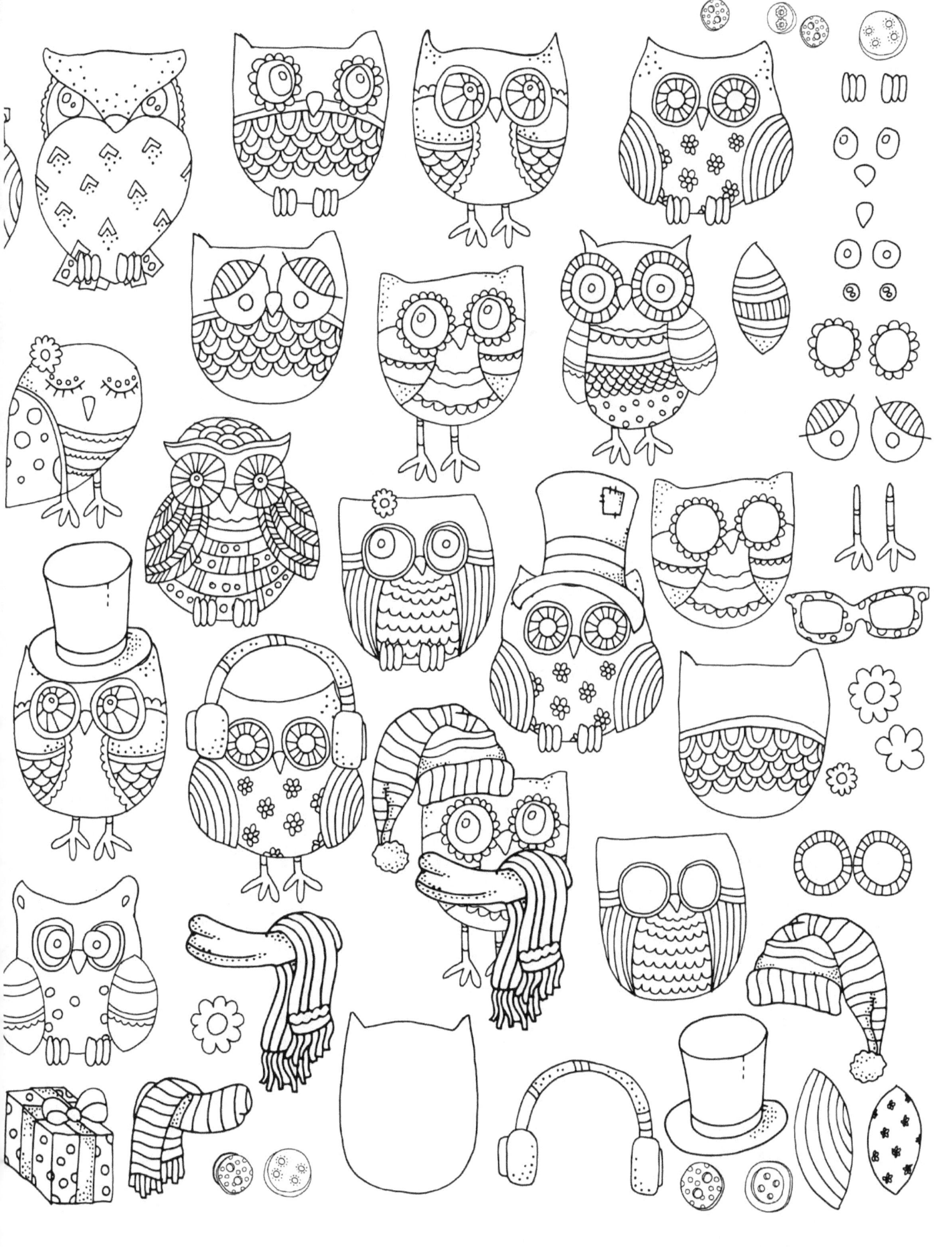

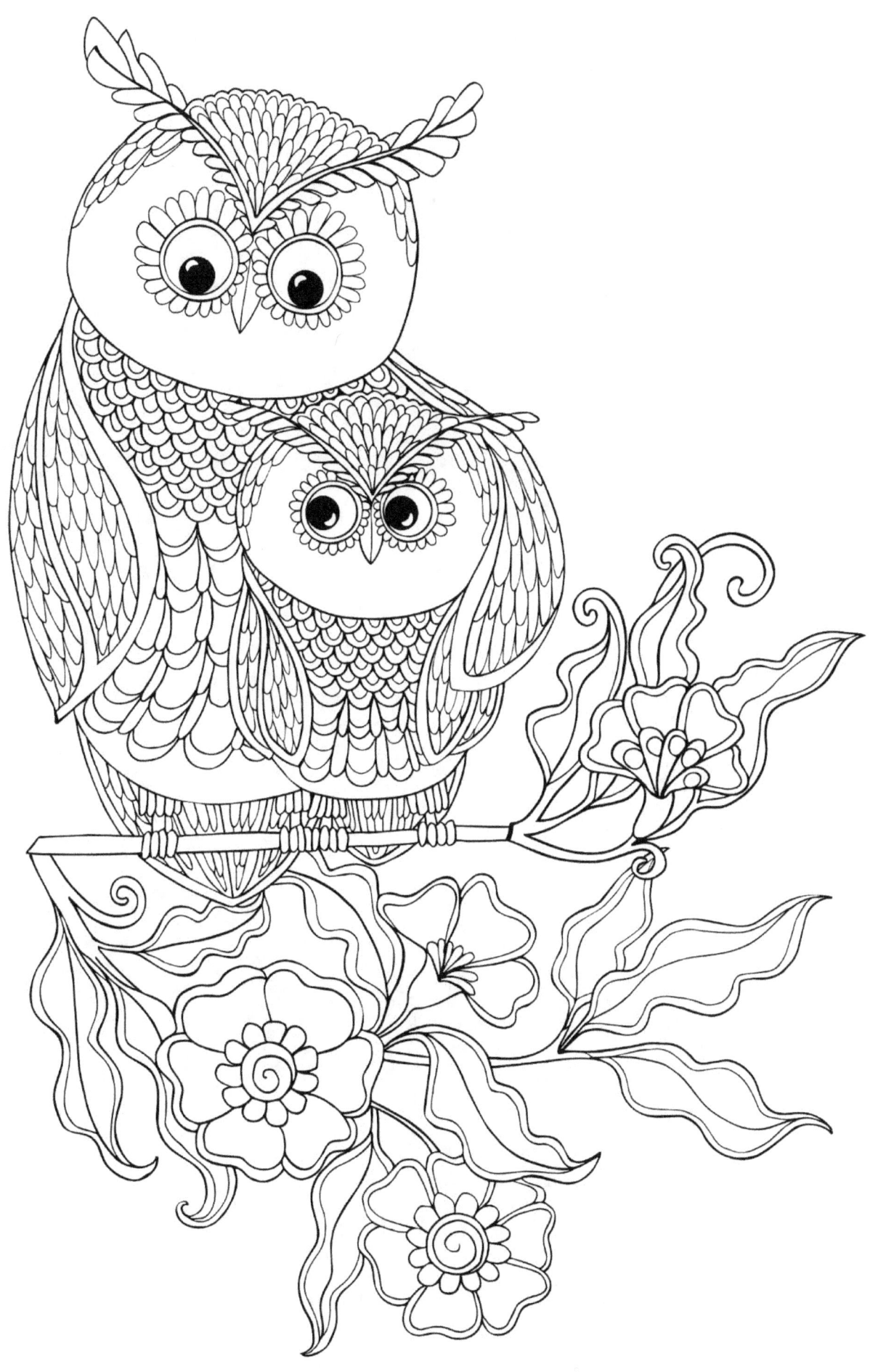

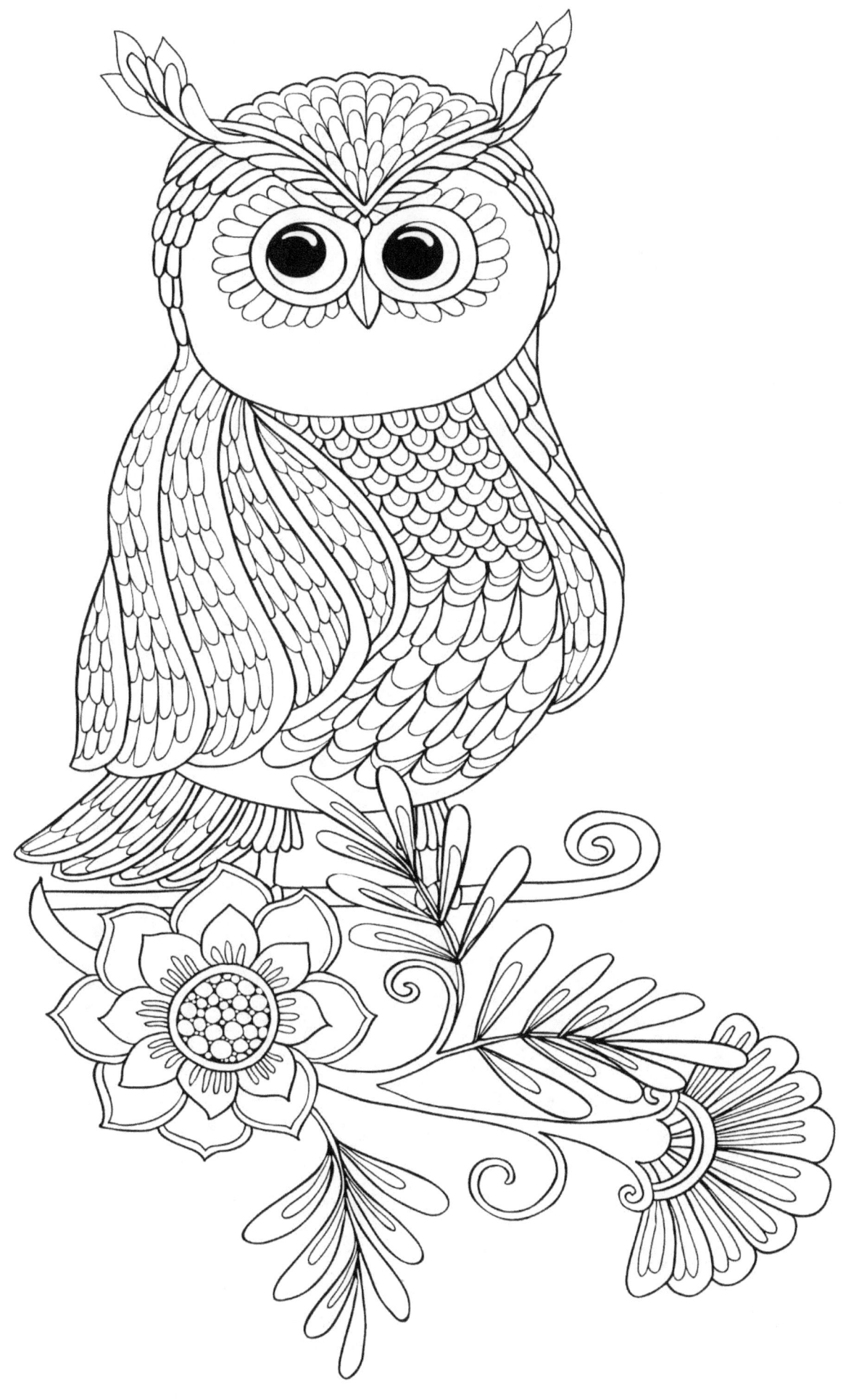

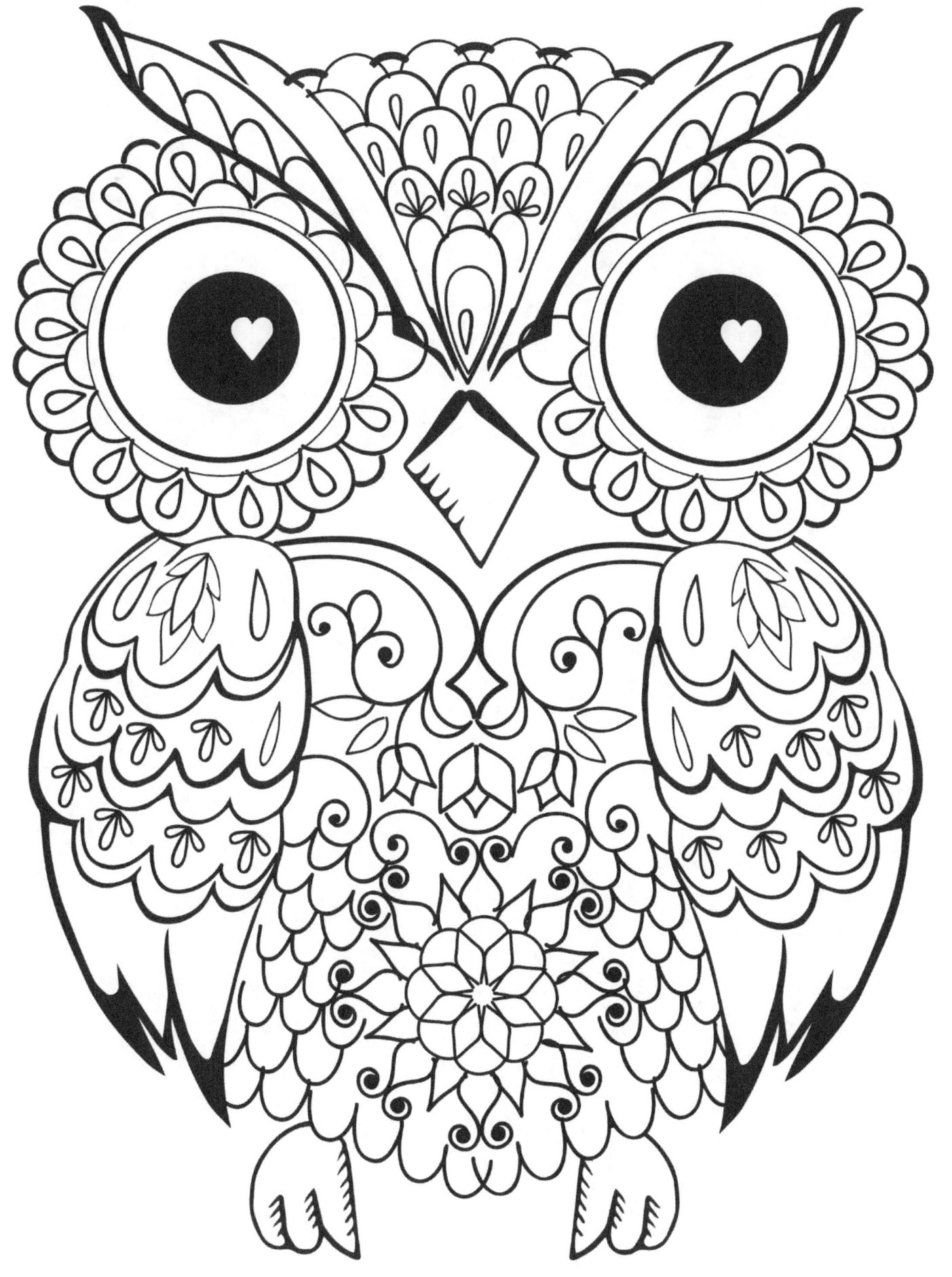

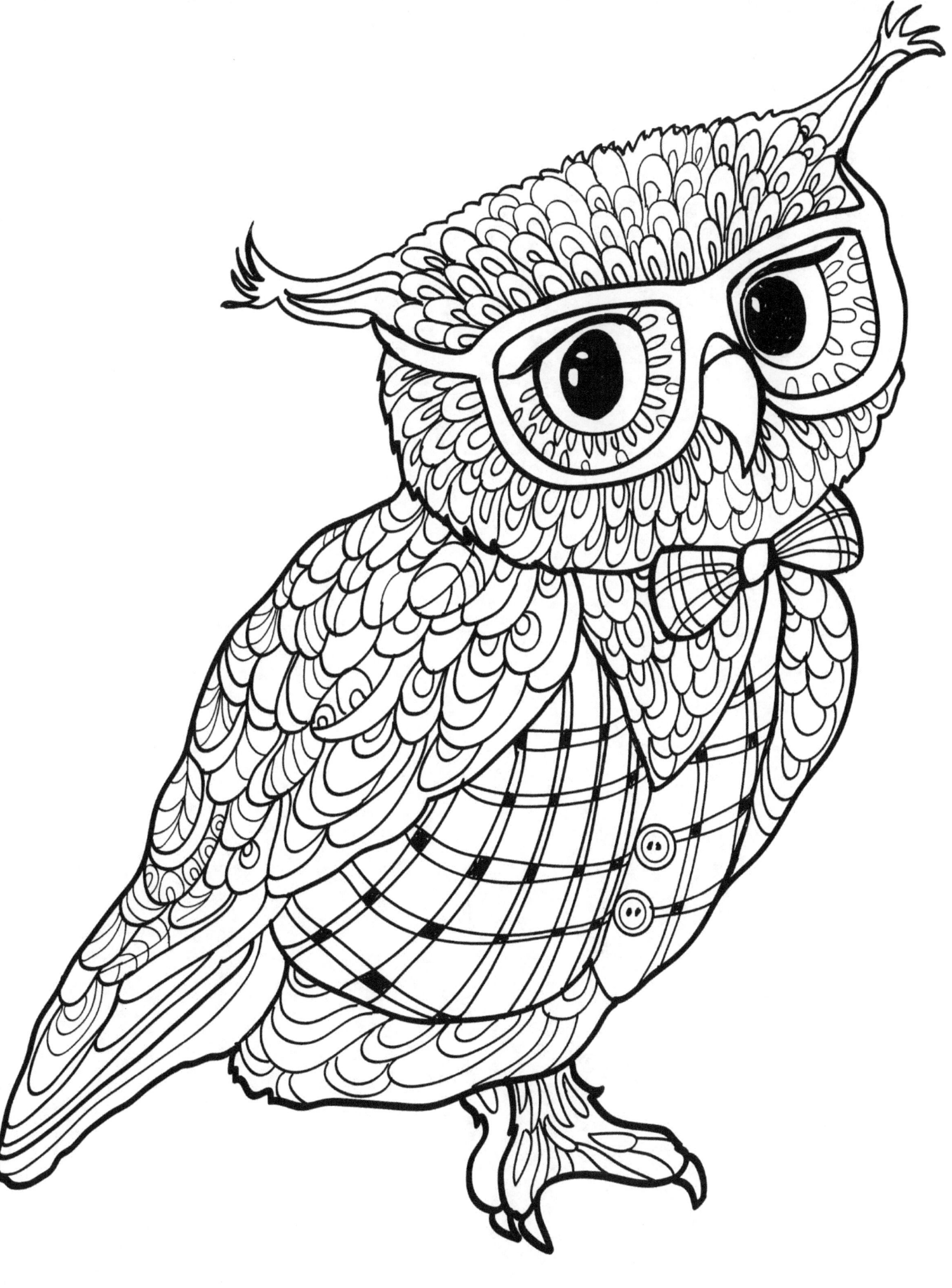

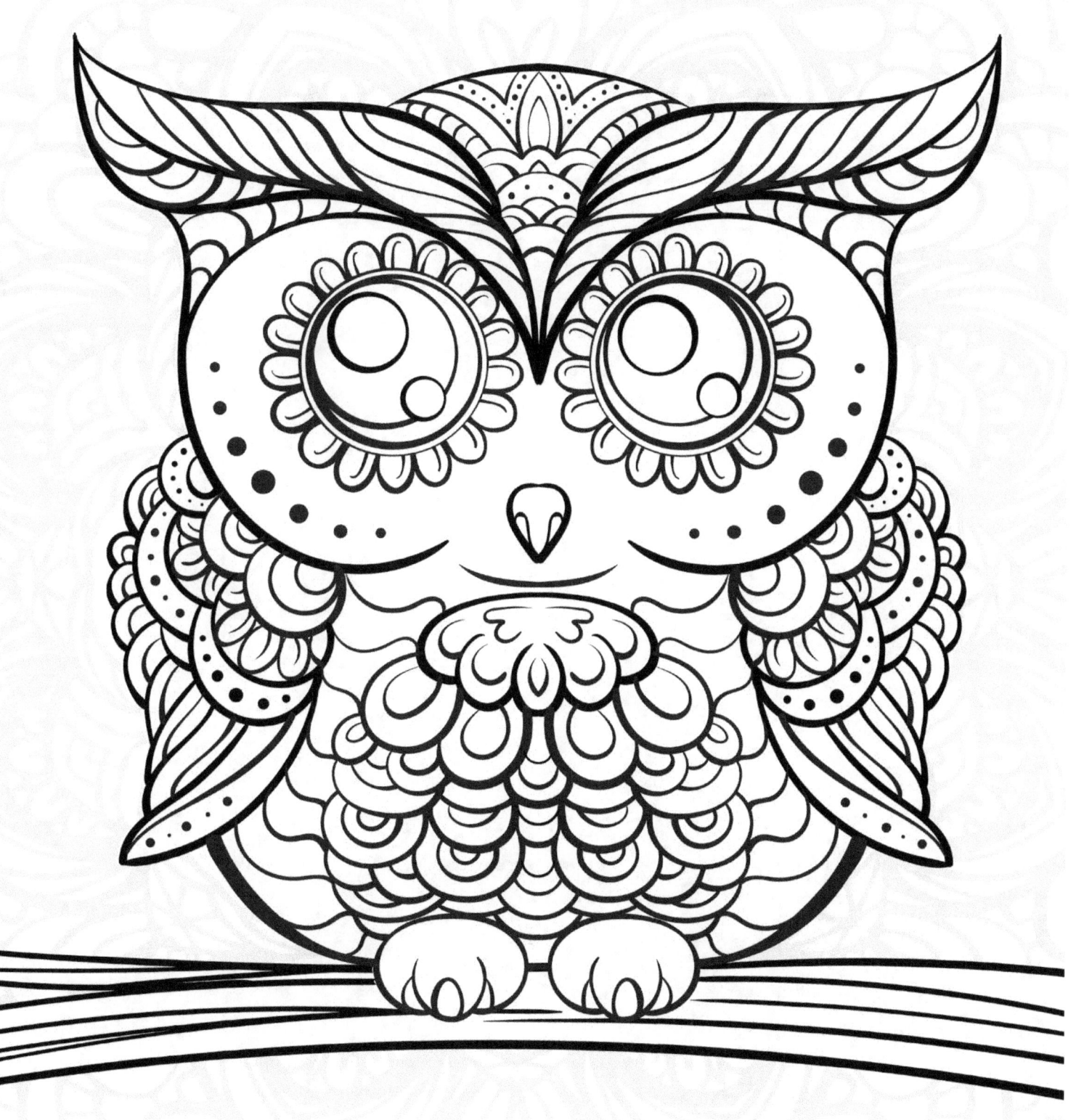

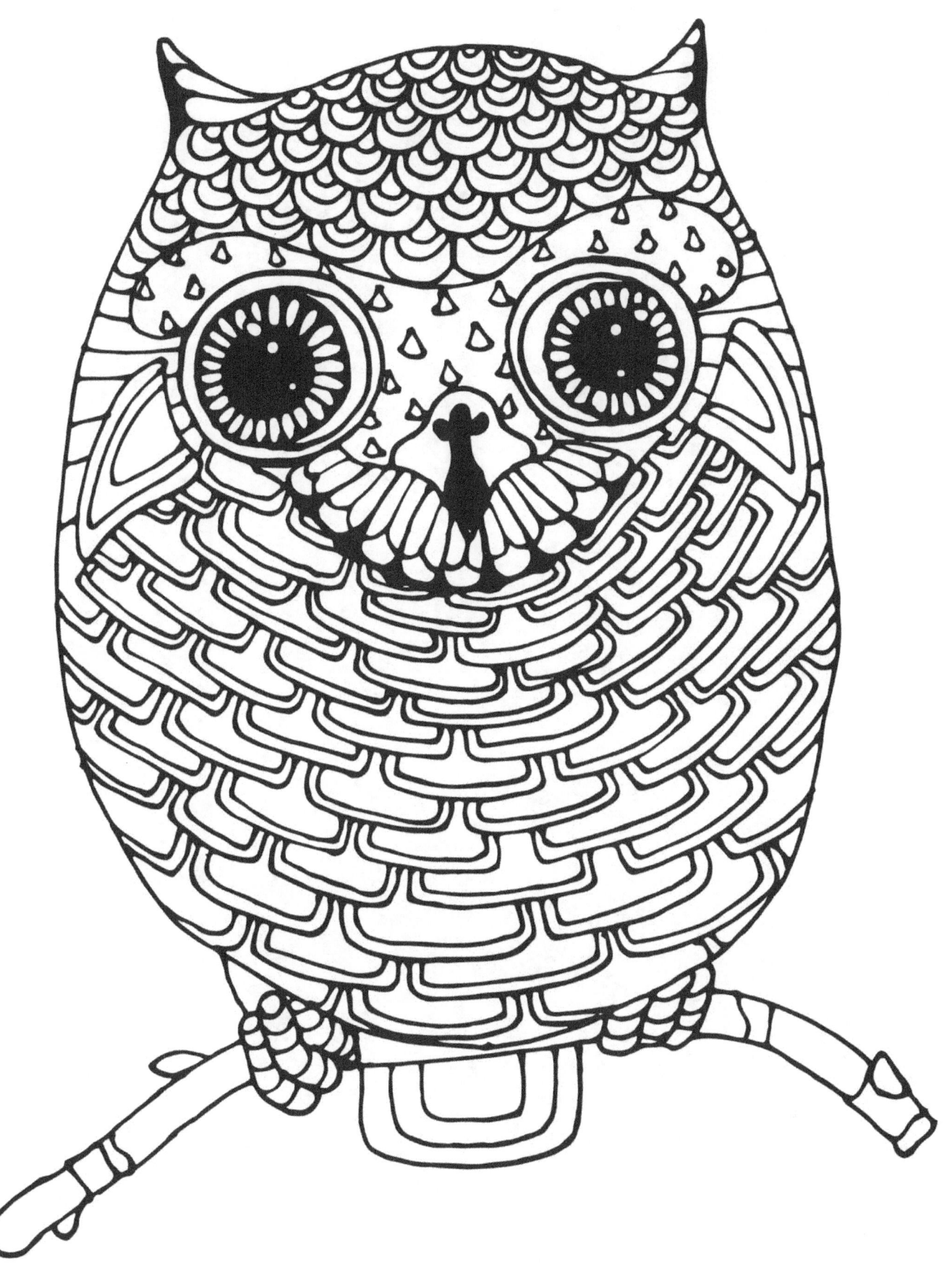

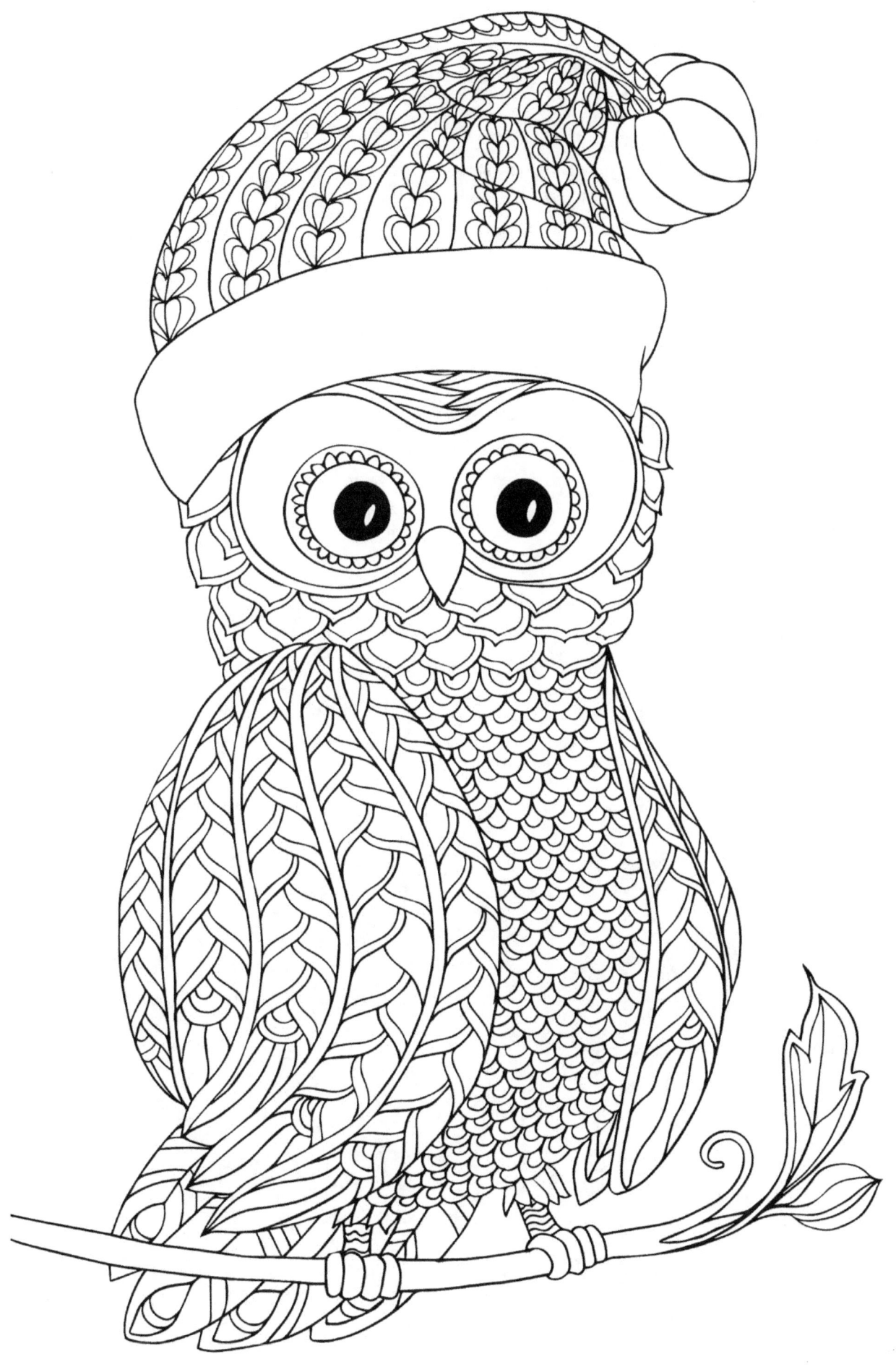

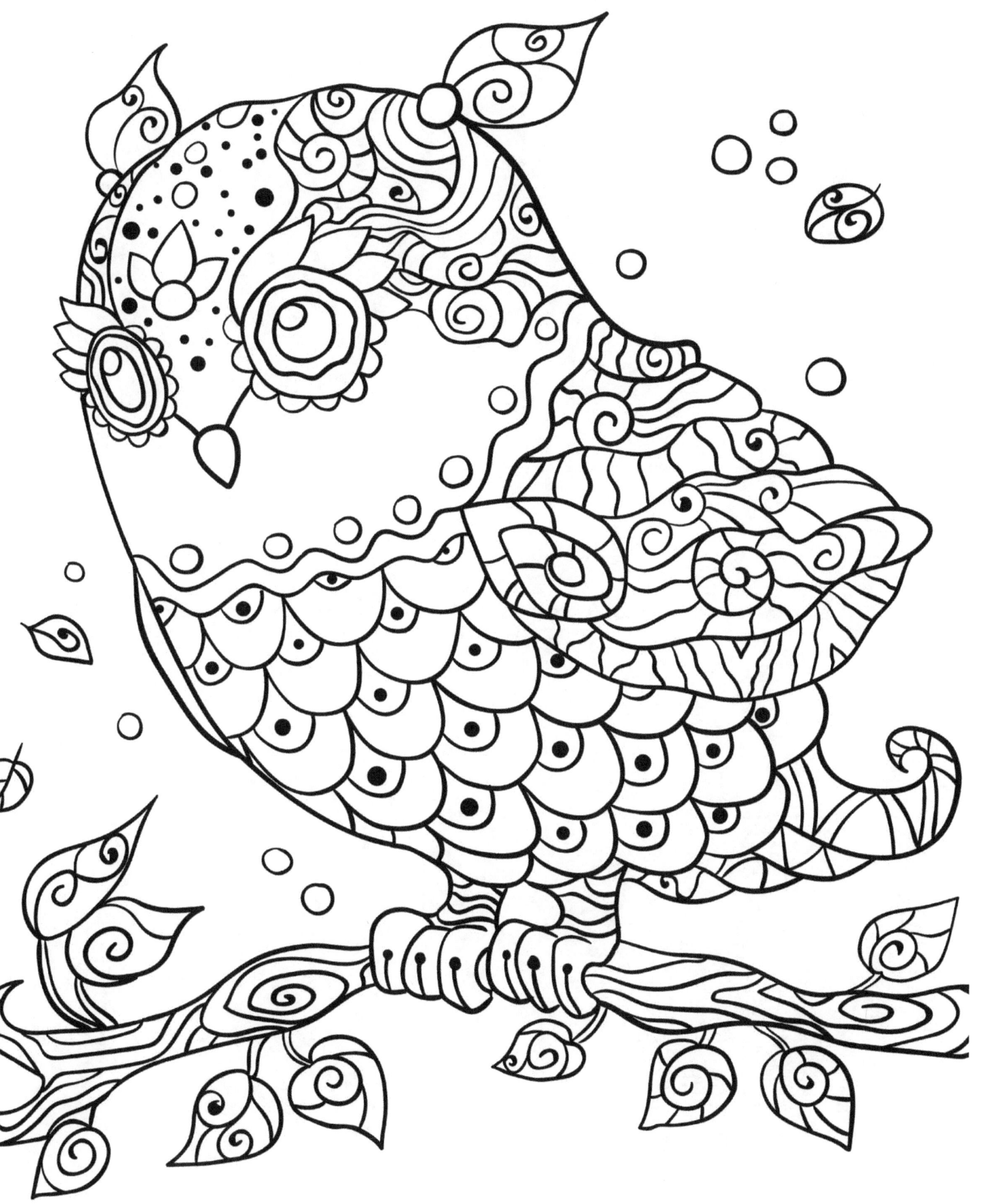

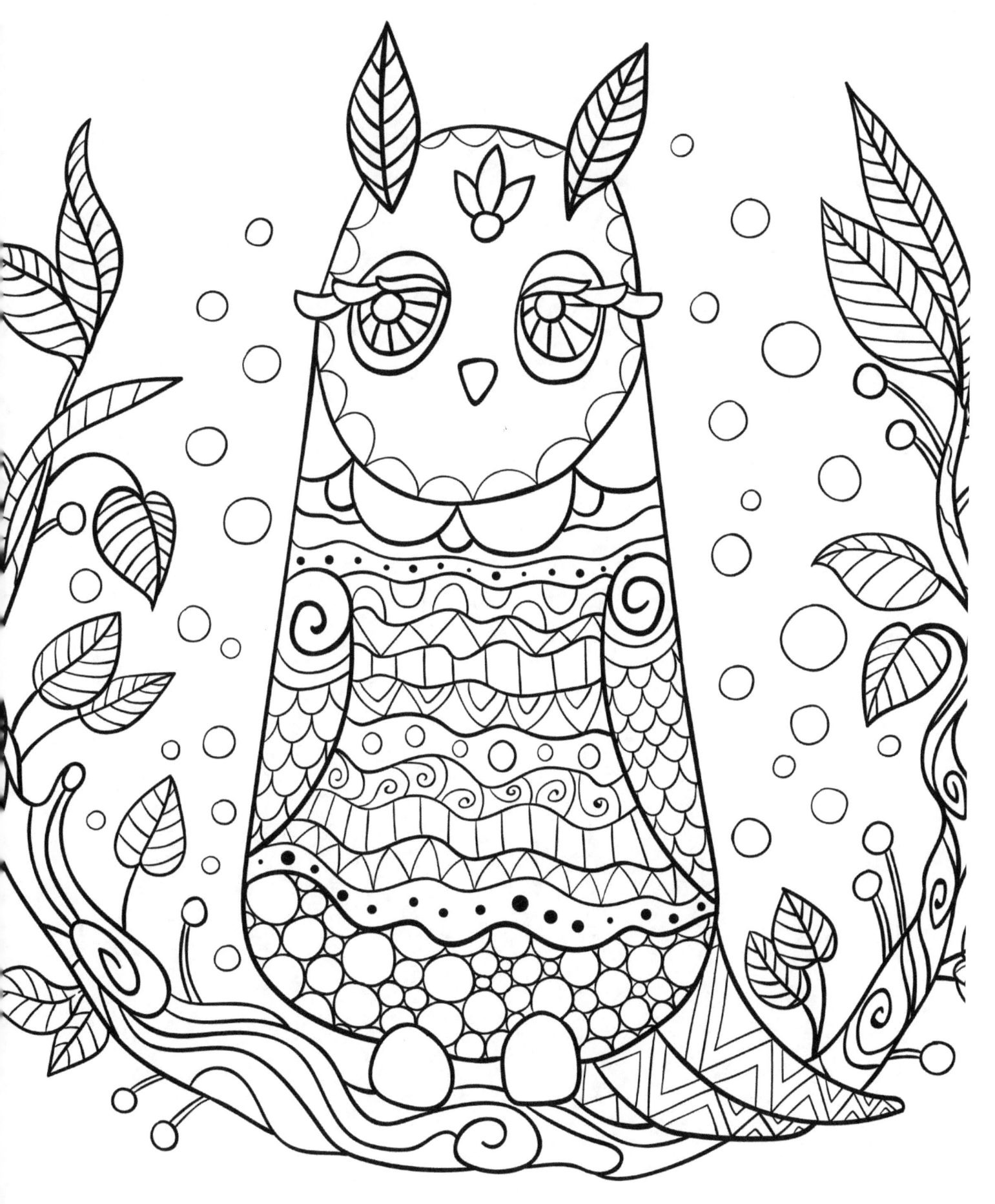

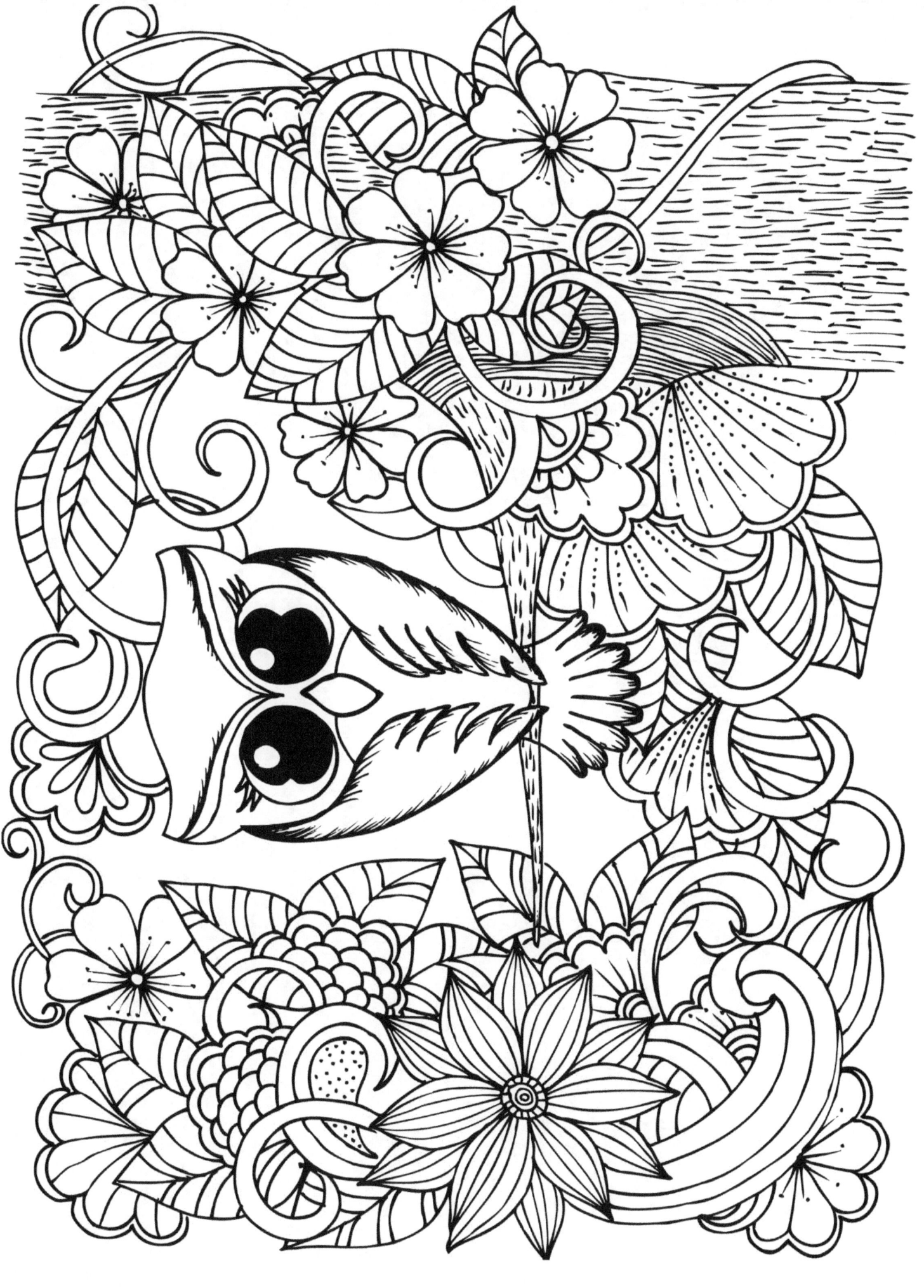

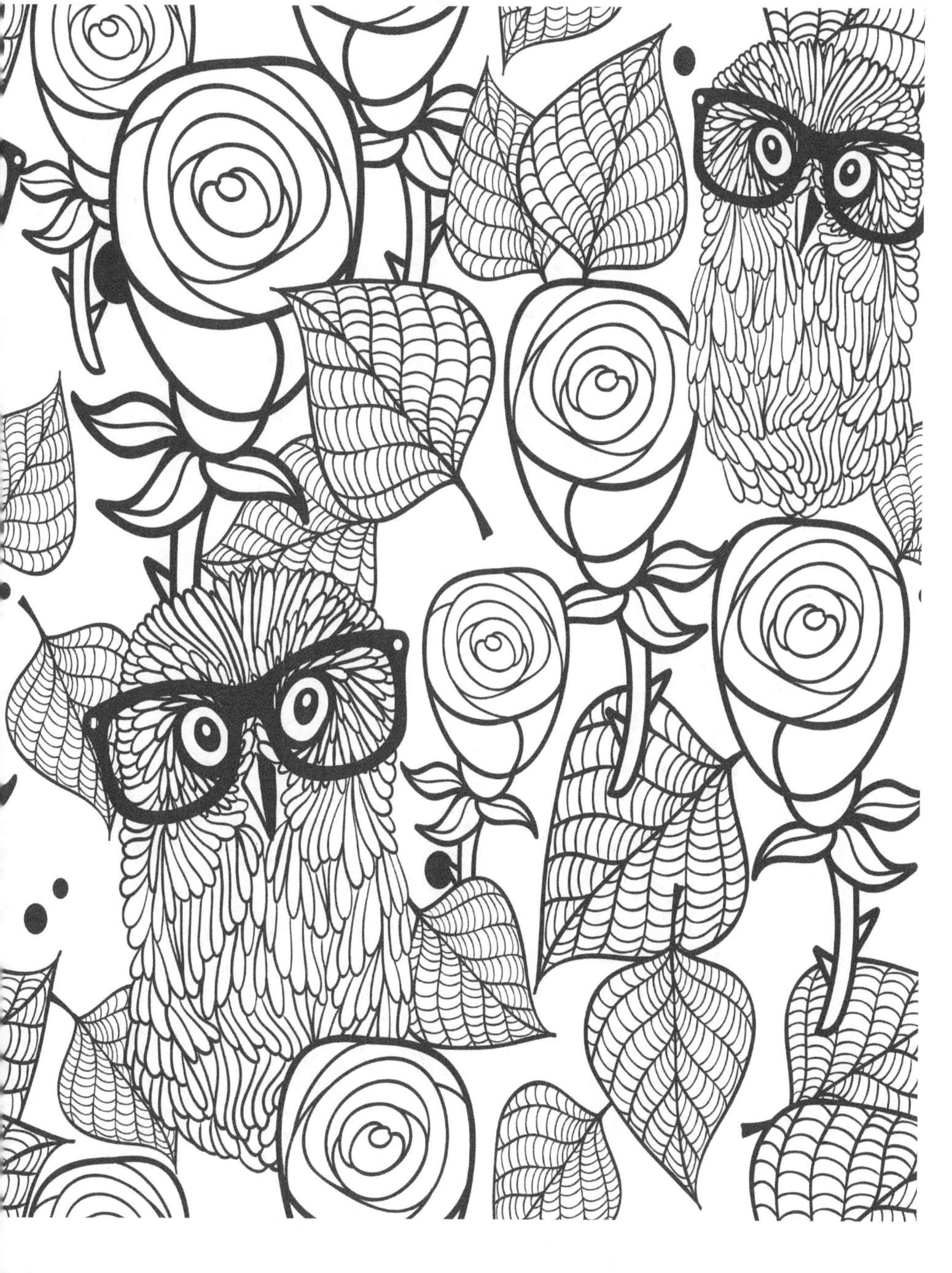

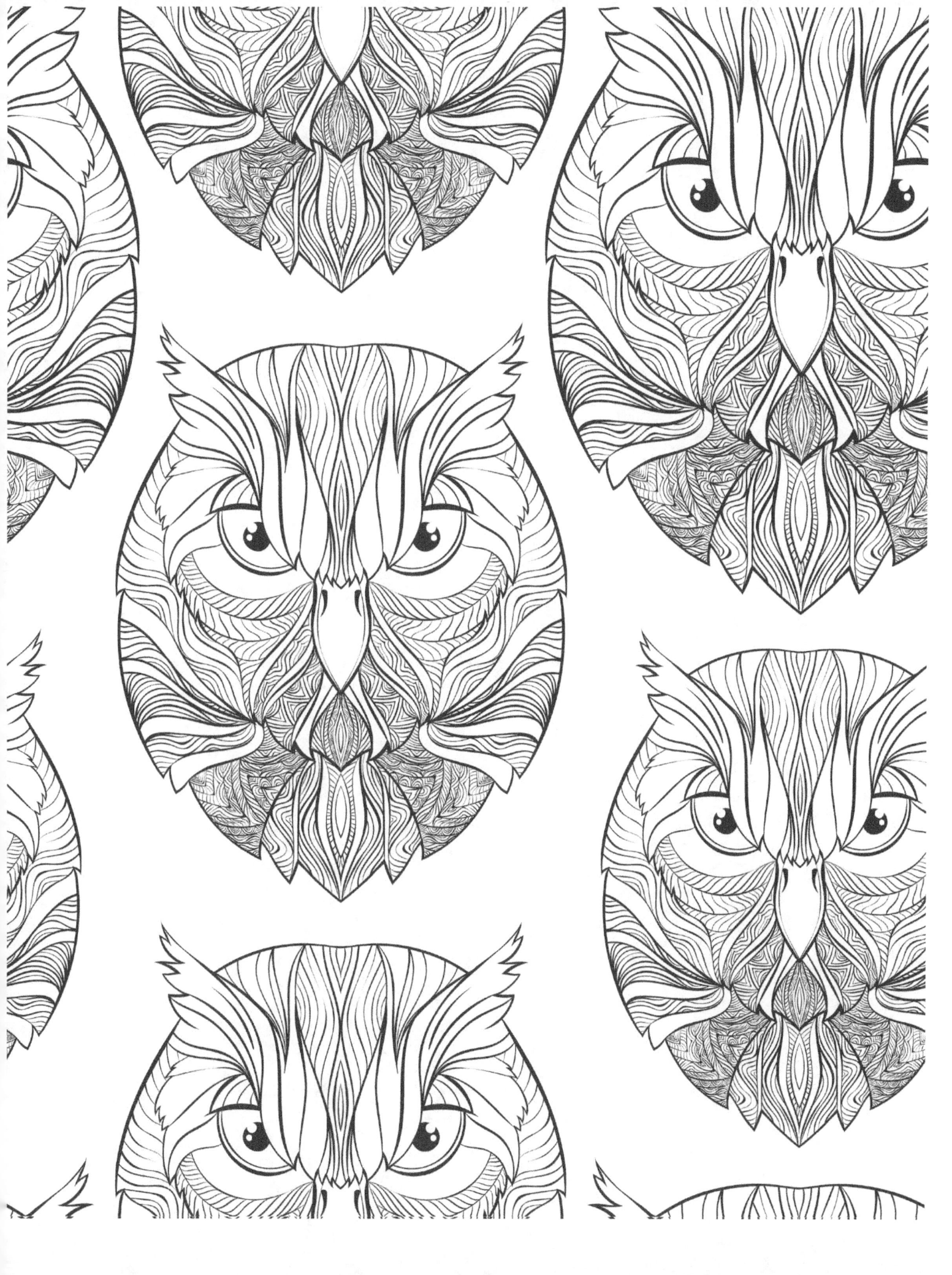

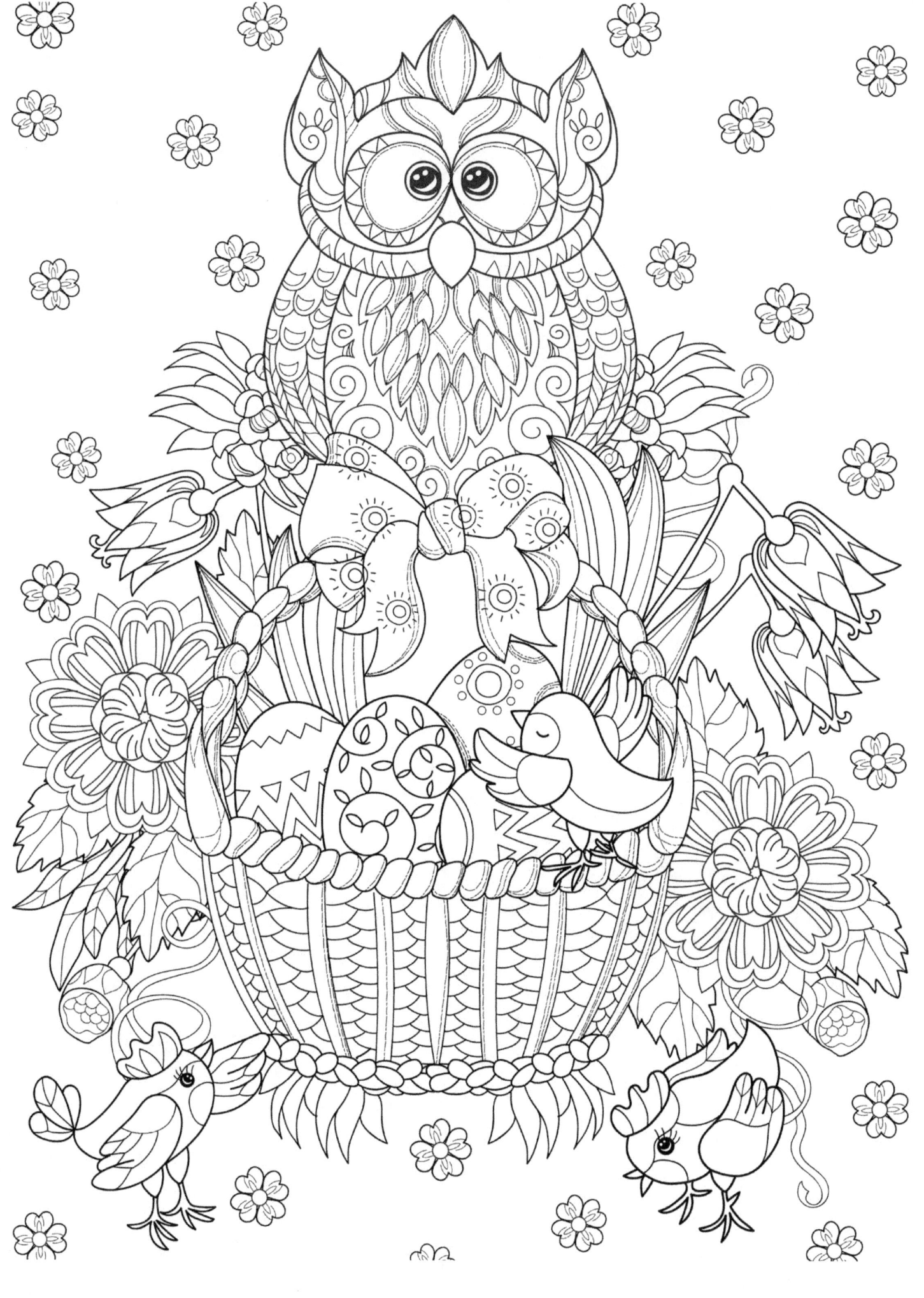

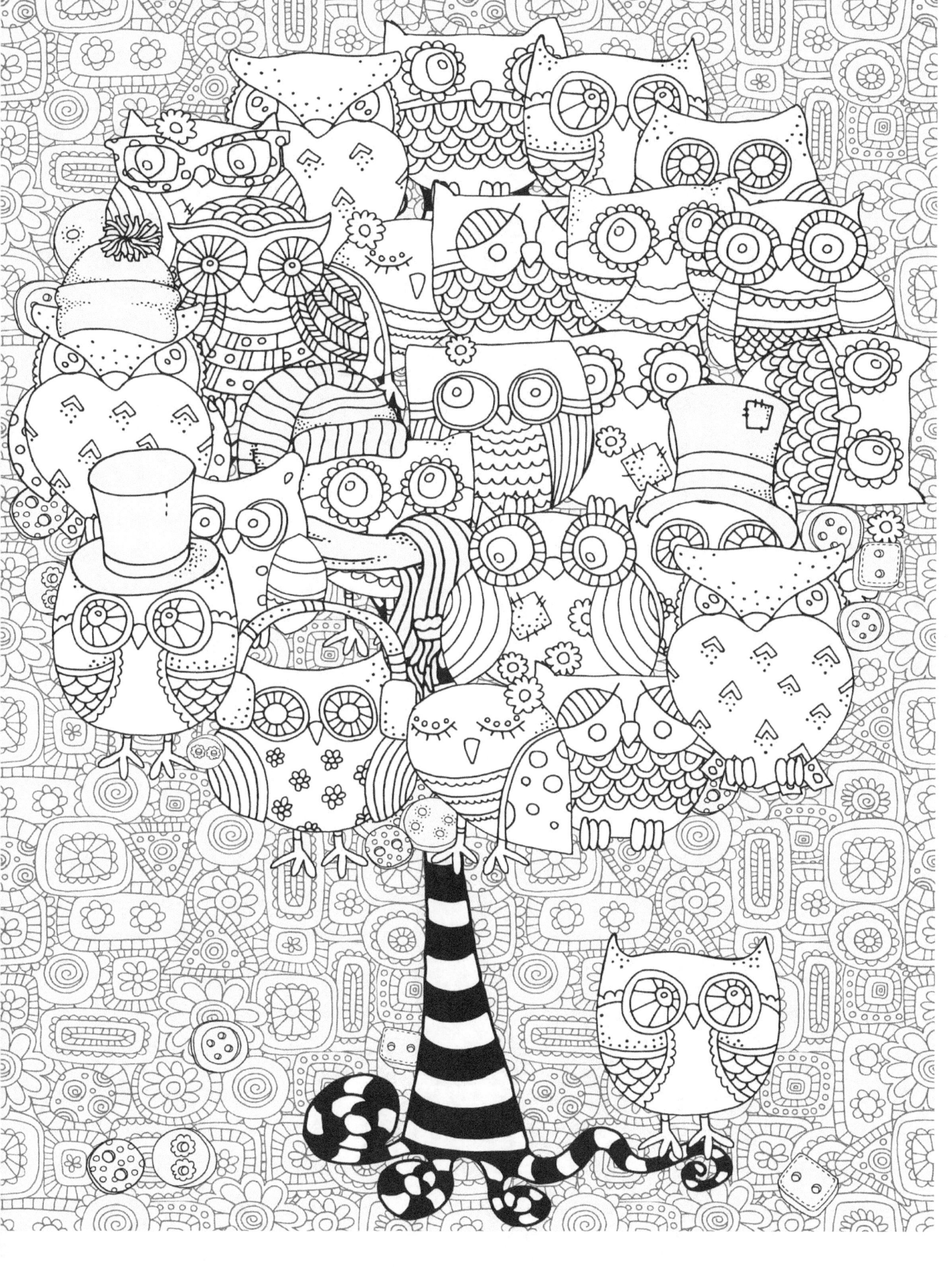

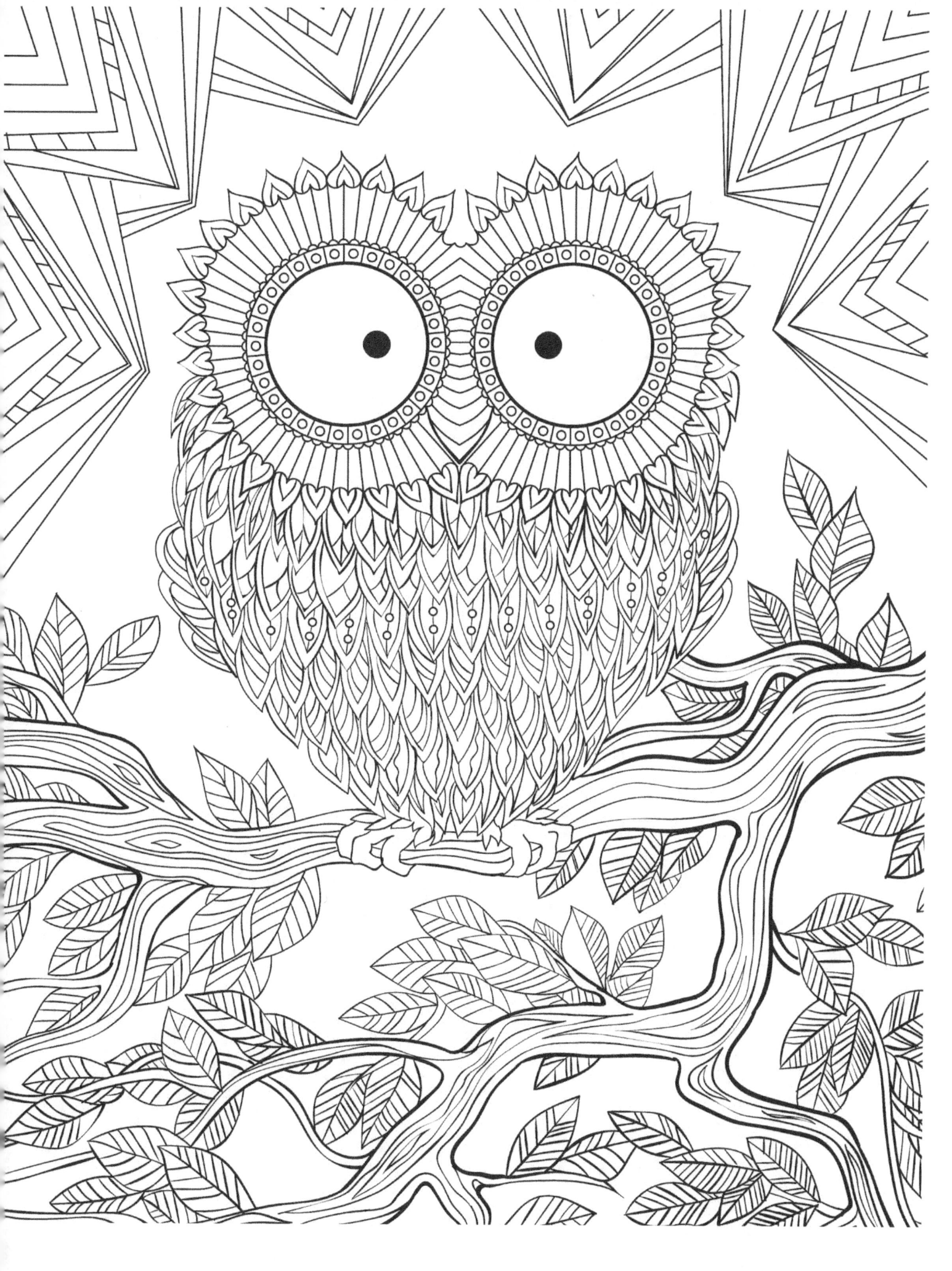

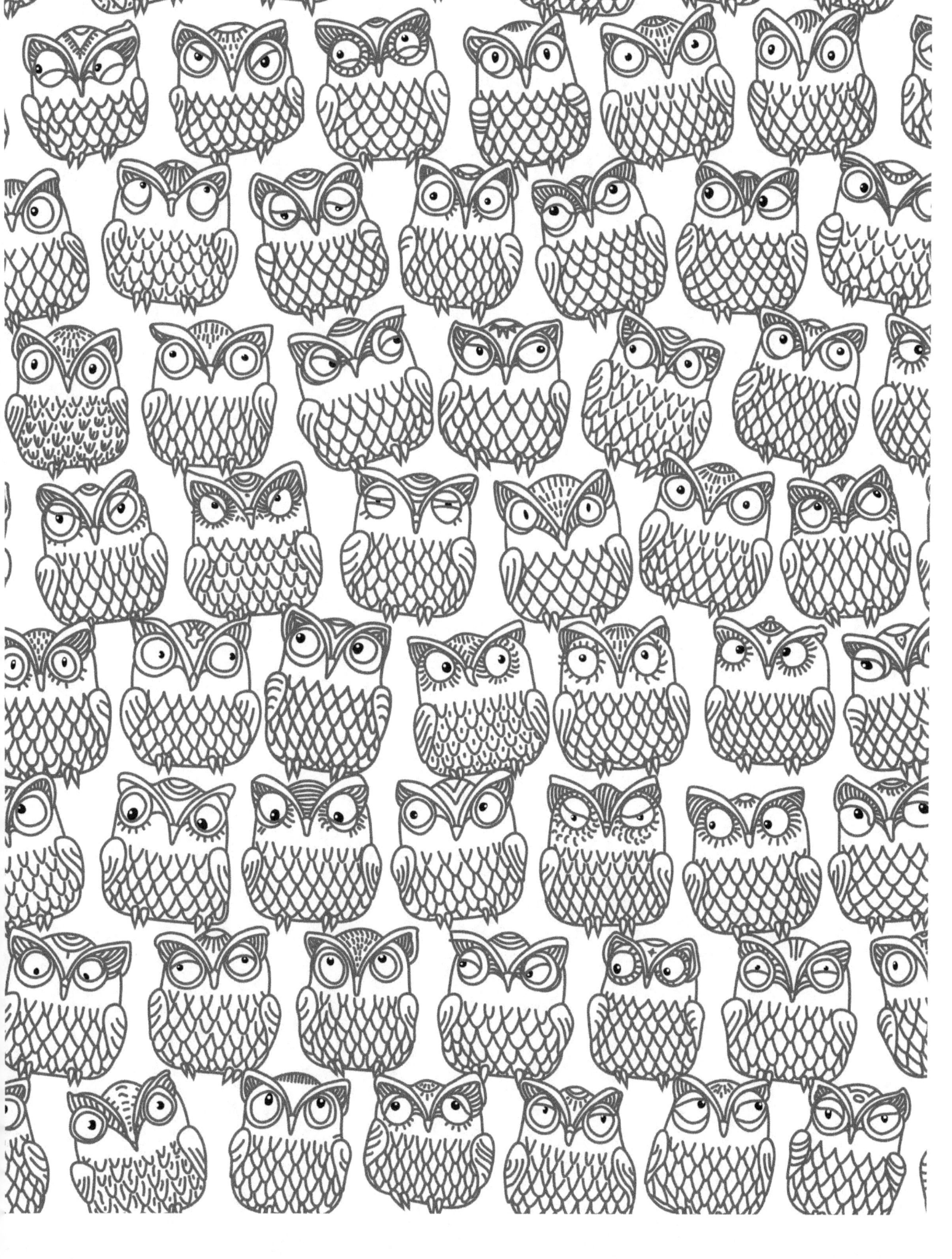

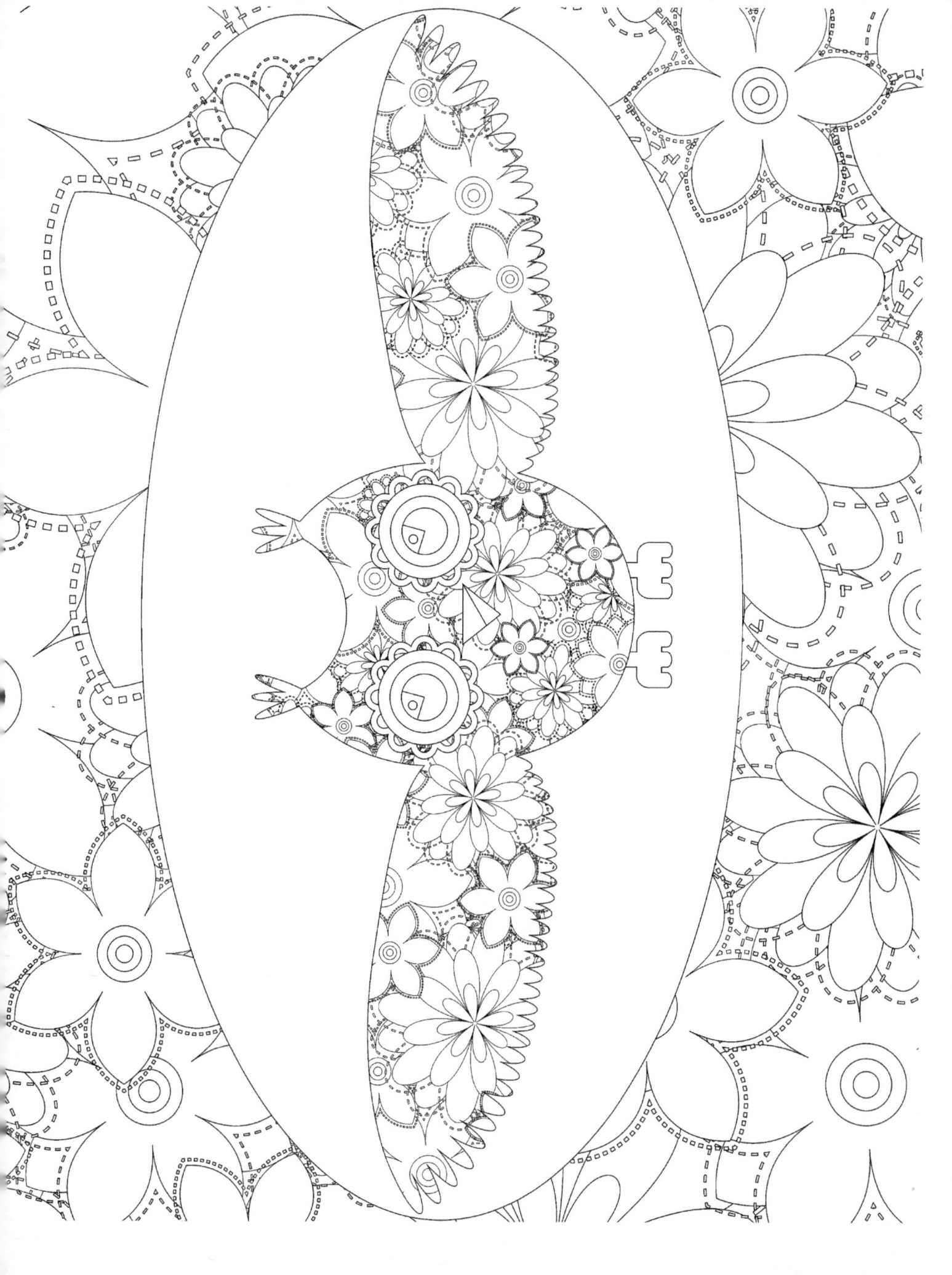